Praise

"Inspiring . . . insightful . . . and extremely helpful. A book I highly recommend every Christian read."

—Dr. Johnny Hunt

"The church desperately needs refocusing therapy—not more focus groups, but missional refocusing. *ONE Focus Living* is what I've been waiting for—a charter and chart for refocusing life and church on what really matters."

—Dr. Leonard Sweet
Best-selling Author and Professor at
Drew University and George Fox University

"The solution to the challenges we face as a nation and as a world is Jesus Christ. Only he can transform us into the people we were created and destined to be by the One who made us. Yes, people need information, but it is the power of Christ exhibited through the lives of his followers in everyday life that causes the world to sit up and take notice. I am thankful for Scotty Sanders and his commitment to pushing us out of our comfort zones and into our neighborhoods and cities to share the love of Jesus. *ONE Focus Living* will bless you, encourage you, and challenge you to take seriously the call of Jesus to love and serve your world."

—Toby Slough
Senior Pastor, Cross Timbers Community Church,
Argyle, Texas

"Scotty Sanders has been successful in helping churches utilize resources, staff and congregation to their fullest potential. One of these tools is *ONE Focus Living*, a book written to inspire and encourage the reader to overcome their fears and insecurities of telling others about their faith in Jesus Christ. This book is not about religion but about *relationship*. ONE Focus Living is part of the ONE Focus Initiative that is storming into churches and setting people's hearts on fire with the passion to reach others for Christ."

—Suellen Roberts
Founder and President, Christian Women in Media

"I have had the privilege of knowing Scotty since 1996 as a personal friend. I have never worked with anyone who had a greater passion for fulfilling his call than Scotty. His insight and knowledge of leadership amaze me. He was intentional and missional in every moment I served with him. The same passion he brought to work every day, he brings to *ONE Focus Living*. I am certain you will enjoy his book, but far more important for Scotty is that you will be challenged to live intentionally for Jesus."

—Dr. David Uth
Senior Pastor, First Baptist Church
Orlando, Florida

"This book will work! *ONE Focus Living* is a practical, doable resource for achieving a lifestyle of evangelism in and through one's daily life because it focuses on doing ONE thing—and that keeps it simple for The Swan! Can you imagine an entire church family focusing on ONE thing, like evangelism? Well, get yourself a cup of java and enjoy! Your ability to do ONE thing well is about to take 'focus' in your life and church!"

—Dr. Dennis Swanberg
America's Minister of Encouragement

"For too long most Christians have been content to sit on the sidelines rather than share their faith. *ONE Focus Living* gives each of us a plan to get in the game and be an impact player!"

—Andrew Whitworth
Offensive tackle, NFL Cincinnati Bengals

"We are called to love one another as Christ loves us, which is easy for our hearts to understand but often a work-in-progress in our humanness. *ONE Focus Living* provides guidance on nurturing genuine, intimate interaction without superficiality or surface talk. As an actress who desires to inspire audiences through cinema, I am filled with the giddiest joy as I make lifelong friendships and share in the fruits of that friendship."

—Jenn Gotzon
Actress, Frost/Nixon, Doonby, God's Country,
Alone Yet Not Alone, Dragon Day

"One Lord, one faith—reaching one person at a time! *ONE Focus Living* is an inspiring new book by Scotty Sanders designed to do just that!"

—Dr. Frank Hoffmann
Louisiana state representative

"*ONE Focus* is equipping people to engage ONE unchurched person by sharing the love of Jesus for one year. Should you do this? Absolutely! Anything that can help you reach people for the Lord Jesus Christ—you ought to be doing it. This is a nonconfrontational, missional outreach. You don't have to set out to share the Gospel. It doesn't have to be one-on-one. You're just developing a relationship and sharing the love of Jesus. Why wouldn't you want to do this? Absolutely be part of it. It's doable by everyone."

—Dr. Steve James,
Senior pastor, Trinity Baptist Church
Lake Charles, Louisiana

"In my twenty-one years as director of evangelism, I have seen only a few ministries that have impacted churches like *ONE Focus*. The concept is simple, biblical, and transferable. It has the capability of changing the culture of the church."

—Dr. Wayne Jenkins,
Director of church growth and evangelism, Louisiana Baptist Convention

"Each week, more and more introduce their friends and neighbors to me who are their ONEs."

—Dr. Waylon Bailey,
Senior pastor, First Baptist Church
Covington, Louisiana

"I want to endorse Scotty Sanders, Mike Walker, and *ONE Focus*. *ONE Focus* has allowed Summer Grove Baptist Church to rally around the Great Commission and to give each member a way to reach out to another unchurched individual. I would strongly suggest that you consider *ONE Focus* as you join me in praying for a great awakening."

—Dr. Rod Masteller,
President, Louisiana Baptist Convention
Senior pastor, Summer Grove Baptist Church
Shreveport, Louisiana

"I am so excited about *ONE Focus*. In it, God has given us a very clear plan for evangelism. *ONE Focus* has moved our people out of their comfort zones to love and disciple their friends and to lead them to a personal relationship with Jesus Christ."

—Kevin Cottrell
Pastor of missions/evangelism, First Baptist Church
Broken Arrow, Oklahoma

"*ONE Focus* allowed our whole church to get on the same page for an entire year."

—Mark Fenn
Global ministries pastor, First Baptist Church
West Monroe, Louisiana

"As the pastor of a 175-year-old church, I was looking for something that would move personal evangelism to the top of the church's priorities. *ONE Focus* met my requirements and more. People are talking about their ONEs at church and in the community. We are on pace to baptize more than any time in my pastorate, and most of them were led to Christ by members of the church and not the staff. Use the material, follow the guidelines, and reap the harvest."

—Dr. Terry Bostick
Senior pastor, First Baptist
Oxford, Alabama

"ONE Focus inspires, equips, and encourages disciples to move from spectators to active participants in the Great Commission. Anchored in prayer and the power of God, this initiative has lifted the sights of our members and catalyzed new enthusiasm for outreach. ONE Focus has put legs on our vision to be a church without walls. Few things you ever do . . . will have the impact of ONE Focus!"

—Art McNeese
Senior pastor, BridgeWay Church
Copper Canyon, Texas

"While the ONE Focus concept is simple, making it happen is not. ONE Focus provides us with all the tools we need to effectively share this simple vision . . . and see it become a reality."

—Philip Robertson
Senior pastor, Philadelphia Baptist Church
Deville, Louisiana

"The best aspect of ONE Focus is the simplicity of picking ONE and placing an emphasis on reaching that ONE, while still being sensitive and available for others as well. It's not age-specific, so all ages are able to participate in the Great Commission. Our ONE Focus launch resulted in 87 percent commitment from our church, but I did not have my own ONE until I got a call about a neighbor in the midst of a crisis. After meeting with this young man, I knew he was to be my ONE. He called this week and is coming to church on Sunday."

—Bill Reid
Senior pastor, Calvary Baptist
Ruston, Louisiana

"What an incredible year! Baptisms are up over a previous year's high. We had 116 commitments of faith on the closing Sunday of *ONE Focus*. Thank you for your encouragement and continued desire to see the lost come to know Jesus as Savior."

—Greg Bath
Missions/evangelism pastor, Trinity Baptist
Lake Charles, Louisiana

"People are praying each day for their ONE. Just recently, I had a young teenage church member tell me, 'I think my ONE is getting close to accepting Christ. God has already given me my next ONE!'"

—John Mark Little
Senior pastor, Victory Baptist
Monroe, Louisiana

"*ONE Focus* is clearly a movement of God in our church. Ninety-eight percent of our attending members committed to ONE. Our members are praying and reaching out to their ONEs and God is providing opportunities. With the *ONE Focus* Initiative and much prayer and commitment, we've had a tremendous response. Will you love ONE for a year?"

—Cyle Clayton
Senior pastor, Calvary Baptist
Many, Louisiana

"We saw the greatest improvements in children and youth departments with *ONE Focus*. Both departments doubled in size. Wednesday night attendance jumped as well. It's great to see the church so involved in Kingdom work. We've had great results with baptisms, doubling our previous year."

—Dominick DiCarlo
Senior pastor, First Baptist Church
Jena, Louisiana

"Anything that can engage most or all of the church in evangelism has to be good. During *ONE Focus* we saw baptisms rise over 700 percent compared to the previous year's report."

—Wayne Gray
Senior pastor, Ferriday Baptist Church
Ferriday, Louisiana

"From the first time I heard Scotty Sanders share the vision of *ONE Focus*, I knew that it would change me and my ministry. After arriving at First Baptist Church of Mount Olive, I shared the vision of *ONE Focus* with my pastor and staff. From the time we made the commitment to go forward with ONE, momentum began building. This change in momentum began to be seen in increased Sunday school and worship attendance, more first-time and repeat visitors, renewed energy and enthusiasm in worship, decisions during the invitation time, and increased offerings. Commitment Sunday was more that we could ask for or imagine. Ninety-eight percent of our attending members made a personal commitment to *ONE Focus* on commitment Sunday. We have been more than pleased with the resources and personal coaching from Scotty Sanders, Mike Walker, and the *ONE Focus* team. I recommend *ONE Focus* to you and your church."

—Scott Harmon
Minister of education, First Baptist Church
Mount Olive, Alabama

"We're grateful to the Lord for his leading our church to partner with *ONE Focus*. There's a renewed spirit of anticipation that permeates throughout our church family. We're seeing people come to faith in Christ every week. We heartily recommend Scotty, Mike, and the rest of the Life Catalyst team."

—Ken Schroeder
Senior pastor, First Baptist Church
Mandeville, Louisiana

"I was amazed at what God did during our commitment service for *ONE Focus* this past Sunday. How wonderful it is to see our church looking for a person they can influence for Jesus!"

—Dr. E. Whit Holmes
Senior pastor, Parkview Baptist
Monroe, Louisiana

"*ONE Focus* has been absolutely worth it. We would do it again. Approximately 80 percent of our people have committed to reach one person for Christ. Our baptisms are up 140 percent over last year because of our people's commitment to *ONE Focus*."

—Lamar Huffman
Senior pastor, Trinity Baptist
Sulphur, Louisiana

"*ONE Focus* ignited our church. As a pastor, I've never experienced the commitment our people now have to doing their parts in the fulfillment of the Great Commission."

—Brad Marchman
Senior pastor, Lawrence Drive Baptist Church
Macon, Georgia

"*ONE Focus* has kept our people focused on those who need to know Christ. We baptized nine times the number [we baptized] last year and the harvest isn't over yet."

—Milton Wilson
Senior pastor, First Baptist Church
LeCompte, Louisiana

"Lots of God things happening through *ONE Focus*—the numbers are very telling: new members up 107 percent; baptisms up 59 percent; Sunday school attendance up 190 people; worship attendance up 32 percent."

—Dr. Chuck Pourciau
Senior pastor, Broadmoor Baptist Church
Shreveport, Louisiana

"Scotty wants to call *ONE Focus* an initiative. He is right. *ONE Focus* encourages members to take the initiative to focus on someone who needs Christ. You can call it whatever you like, but it changes the culture of the church. . . . It gives you a vision to rally around."

—Dr. Charles Wesley
Senior pastor, First Baptist Church
Jonesboro, Louisiana

ONE FOCUS
LIVING

Reaching the World
by Reaching One

SCOTTY SANDERS

ONE Focus Living: Reaching the World by Reaching One

All Scripture quotations are taken from the *Holy Bible, New
International Version*. *NIV*. Copyright © 1973, 1978, 1984 by
International Bible Society. Used by permission of Zondervan.
All rights reserved.

Brown Christian Press
16250 Knoll Trail Drive, Suite 205
Dallas, Texas 75248
www.BrownChristianPress.com
(972) 381-0009

A New Era in Publishing™

ISBN: 978-1-61254-017-7
Library of Congress Control Number 2011932333

Printing in the United States
10 9 8 7 6 5 4 3 2 1

For more information, please visit www.OneFocusLiving.com.

Cindy and I want to dedicate this book to our family,
who has loved, supported, and encouraged us through
every endeavor in life.

Especially to our children:

To our daughter, Jenny Sanders LoBello, for wisdom
beyond her years and a sensitive heart for people, which
draws them to her for counsel and friendship.

To our son, Jacob Sanders, for his gentle spirit, generous heart,
and unique personality that makes everyone feel special.

And to our four precious granddaughters.
Abby Grace LoBello, Ashlyn Rose LoBello, Jillian Kate
Sanders, and Jessa-Claire Sanders, you have given us more love
than we could ever imagine and more "focus" to leave this
world a better place for you and for others!

"We will tell the next generation the praiseworthy
deeds of the Lord, his power and the wonders he has done. . . .
He commanded our forefathers to teach their children, so the
next generation would know them, even the children yet to be
born, and they in turn would tell their children."
—*Psalm 78:4-6*

ONE by ONE by ONE . . .

CONTENTS

ACKNOWLEDGMENTS

One of my greatest honors was to serve and lead these incredible servants of God. Their faith and commitment was instrumental in the launching of the ONE Focus Initiative.

First West (First Baptist Church in West Monroe, Louisiana) staff:

- Mark Fenn, one of my greatest encouragers and confidants, as well as a member of the Church Catalyst Board
- Whit Bass
- Chris Burton
- Sue Griffin
- Judy Groll
- Randy Impson
- Gil Martin
- Ashton McIntyre
- Dwight Munn
- Todd Parr
- Debbie Robertson
- Quinn Stanfill
- Woods Watson

These Catalyst churches and pastors, who were willing to take a risk and step out in faith, paved the way for the thousands to follow:

- Calvary Many: Cyle Clayton
- Calvary Ruston: Bill Reid
- First Baptist Church Covington: Dr. Waylon Bailey
- First Baptist Church Ferriday: Wayne Gray
- First Baptist Church Jena: Dominick DiCarlo
- First Baptist Church Jonesboro: Dr. Charles Wesley
- First Baptist Church LeCompte: Milton Wilson
- First Baptist Church Mandeville: Ken Schroeder
- First Baptist Church Mansfield: Roy Miller
- First Baptist Church Swartz: Jeff Smart
- Parkview Baptist Monroe: Dr. E. Whit Holmes
- Philadelphia Baptist Deville: Philip Robertson
- Summer Grove Baptist Church: Dr. Rod Masteller
- Trinity Baptist Church Lake Charles: Dr. Steve James
- Trinity Baptist Church Sulphur: C. Lamar Huffman
- Victory Baptist Church Monroe: John Mark Little

These were the first two churches to implement ONE Focus by the Life Catalyst Team:

- First Baptist Church in Broken Arrow, Oklahoma: Nick Garland
- First Baptist Church in Longview, Texas: Dr. Tim Watson

Special thanks to my mentor and friend of over twenty years, Marvin Smith. His influence and encouragement in my life will have an impact on the ones God gives me the opportunity to serve.

Special thanks, also, to my dear friend Wayne Jenkins, the director of church growth and evangelism for the Louisiana Baptist Convention. His belief in and support of me were overwhelming. Wayne and his entire team have embraced ONE Focus in every way.

Do not pray for easy lives. Pray to be stronger men.
Do not pray for tasks equal to your powers.
Pray for powers equal to your tasks.
Then the doing of your work shall be no miracle,
but you shall be the miracle.
—Phillips Brooks
1835–1893

Yesterday is gone. Tomorrow has not yet come.
We have only today. Let us begin.
—Mother Teresa
1910–1997

By this all men will know that you
are my disciples, if you love one another.
—Jesus Christ
(John 13:35)

FOREWORD

I am ONE. I was sitting in study hall on a nice spring day in 1975 at Hendersonville High School in the mountains of western North Carolina. Directly in front of me was a pretty blonde-haired girl named Dottie. She turned around and asked me if I would like to come hear her sing at the First Baptist Church. Now, I didn't care much about First Baptist Church, but I cared quite a bit about pretty blonde-haired girls! So for the first time, I found myself sitting in an evangelical church. I didn't know that the revival known as the Jesus Movement was spreading its fire in my little town. That night, I listened to a group of students sing and share about Jesus with a passion I knew nothing about. When they finished, they invited those who wanted to give their lives to Christ to come forward, and when the words of the song invited me to "turn my eyes upon Jesus," I did. At that moment, my eyes were no longer on a pretty girl, but on the great King.

I have never gotten over what happened that night. It has shaped everything in my life. Every good thing I know is because of that night, because one student lived with ONE focus. She was kind. She cared. She risked investing in me. I was her ONE. I thought I might get a date; instead I got life. That's the fruit of ONE Focus living.

Many people have invested in my life through the years, and Scotty Sanders is one of those people. I am where I am today, pastoring one of the great churches in this country, because of Scotty. I really didn't know him well back in 2005. I was serving as the vice president for evangelization at the North American Mission Board (NAMB), and Scotty was the executive pastor at First Baptist Church in West Monroe, Louisiana. He asked me to come speak to the church. Over the next year and a half, he regularly encouraged me to consider the possibility that I was supposed to leave my role at NAMB and come be the senior pastor of this church. I moved from a place of no interest at all to the place I am now—right in the middle of the most fulfilling days of my ministry as I shepherd these wonderful Christ followers. I am thankful to Scotty for that. Before I was even pastor here, I preached as ONE Focus was launched in this church. Five years later, the fruit of ONE continues to be harvested here. And now, through Scotty's leadership, that fruit is being multiplied all over the world. Just like Dottie did for me, ordinary people are finding that they were designed to be partners with Jesus, compelled by his love to care for just one like he did. I am so glad I was somebody's ONE. I am so glad when God leads me to love and share with another the way someone loved and shared with me.

As you read this, you are in a place of incredible opportunity. *ONE Focus living* will enable you to influence others in a way that will still matter in a billion years. The secret that most Christ followers never discover is that when you focus on one, the Great One focuses on you—you are his ONE! The greatest joy, passion, and purpose you will ever know come when you join him in his search for the next life that is ready to be changed. Live with the message of this book for a while. Let it sink into your soul. Then go after ONE Focus living. When you do, you will find you are going after life itself. I know.

I am ONE.

—Dr. John Avant
First Baptist Church in West Monroe, Louisiana

INTRODUCTION

Burning Bush . . . Burning Building . . . Burning Desire
A brief testimony from Scotty Sanders

We all have those points in our lives that define us and change us—usually several over the period of a lifetime. I am no different. When I look back on the past, I can see God laying stepping stones to my current ministry all along my path. The turning point led through burning rubble, but it sparked a fire in my soul.

I was raised as a "good Catholic boy"—I was confirmed in the church and even attended Catholic elementary school. On the inside, however, I knew something was missing. My wife, Cindy, began her personal relationship with Jesus when she was nine years old. She grew up in the Baptist church, never missing a service. Cindy and I began dating at age fifteen. During a revival at First Baptist Church, I realized that although I had been a religious person, I longed for something more. The emptiness was overwhelming. It was at that point I knew I needed a relationship with Jesus Christ.

After Cindy and I were married (by both a Catholic priest and a Baptist preacher!), I attended one year of college, only to decide it was not for me. I did eventually go back to school to earn my undergraduate and master's degrees the hard way—while working full-time at church and raising a family—but at the time, I had already been a part of a successful family business, and I was even named Entrepreneur of the Year. I oversaw ten electronics stores in a three-state area and we were making a good income. I had an eye for business and finance and knew that was my future.

About that time, we joined Cindy's home church. I began to grow and hunger after God's Word. God gave me an insatiable desire to know more about him, and I quickly became involved in leading Sunday school classes. Although my spiritual life seemed to be on the fast track, there was a restlessness in my spirit, which I masked by working harder and harder. I was achieving great financial success, but my home life was suffering.

It was around 2:00 a.m. on August 17, 1986, when I received a call from my brother-in-law, who was also the manager of my store in Jackson, Mississippi. He was distraught as he told me that the store was on fire. The thought that hit me at that moment was, *This could change everything.* I do not remember the details of the two-hour drive, but what I do remember is driving up to the building and seeing the fire still smoldering. It looked like something you would see on TV. The scene was chaotic—firefighters everywhere, news reporters milling around, and a crowd of curious onlookers.

Once the fire was completely extinguished, I walked through the remains of the building, feeling sick to my stomach. Everything was destroyed . . . electronics, desks, files. There was nothing left. The stench is something I will never forget. It was like a terrible dream I just wanted to wake up from.

God had certainly gotten my attention. Even though I was a Christ follower and was active in church by being a small-group teacher and a deacon, I knew that Christ and my family had taken a backseat to my business. God had been gently trying to reorder my priorities but I had not been listening.

The next day, as I contemplated the ramifications of the fire, many years of inner turmoil came to a head. God ripped out of me any desire to put money or business ahead of him. God did a heart operation on me, and I found the thought of chasing the dollar had become revolting. In retrospect, I realize that God allowed this tragedy because he knew it would take a major event to bring me into his will and prepare me for his mission for my life.

God continued to work on my heart over the next two years, and after a series of events, I was ready to sell my multimillion-dollar business. In August 1988, Cindy and I put our house up for sale and said to God, "We will go and do whatever you want." God led me into the ministry, which has included executive and administrative pastor roles at two mega-churches, being a part of the team that developed the ONE Focus initiative, founding a church consulting business (Life Catalyst Consulting), and now writing *ONE Focus Living*. As of this printing, the ONE Focus Initiative has been used or is being used in sixty churches across the United States, and we are having discussions with churches in Canada, Wales, and India, with expectations that it will continue to spread.

For Moses, God used a burning bush; for me, he used a burning building. And from that divinely scheduled appointment, just like Moses, he put in my heart a burning desire to be obedient to God and share his Word.

ONE Focus: An Overview

When Hurricane Katrina struck in 2005, Cindy and I were working at First Baptist Church in West Monroe, Louisiana. This church, known as First West, would become a home to more than two hundred hurting people at any one time in the aftermath of the hurricane, providing for needs ranging from food and shelter to locating family members, from medical issues to finding jobs, from marriages to burials. Out of this devastation, God's grace and power moved us in a mighty way. Our church members and staff learned to shift their focus to the one person being helped, showing God's love to one person at a time in a real, personal way—out of the tragedy of the hurricane, ONE Focus was born.

At its core, ONE Focus is demonstrational evangelism. It is choosing to show God's love to one individual for one year through acts of prayer, friendship, kindness, and compassion. It is more than that, though, because once you seek God's heart and begin to share his love for the lost, you will find yourself living out that love toward the people with whom you live, work, learn, and play—and doing so on a daily basis. ONE Focus is about focusing on one person, but it is also about living as an example to all, a living testament to the Good News.

As believers, we know we are to share God's love with a hurting world, letting Christ shine through us so others may know the hope that we have. But in practice, excuses and obstacles arise; we feel insecure, ill-prepared, unsure, unworthy, or downright uncomfortable with evangelism. We often fail to show God's love to people we see every day.

What if God could use you, regardless of your fears and insecurities? (He can.) What if God specialized in using the unlikeliest of people, in turning the world's outcasts, rejects, or just plain ordinary folks into the instruments of his glory? (He does.) What if people in desperate need of God's saving grace were all around you? (They are.) What if God met you right where you were when you submitted to him, opening doors you never thought possible? (He will.) What if you had the ability, through Christ, to make a major difference in the world? (You do.)

Are you willing and ready to be changed for the better and to spark and inspire change in those around you? I believe God is and has been ready, and he is more than able to use you, no matter how impossible it feels to you. Remember nothing is impossible with God. What if you committed one year to reaching one person with the love of Jesus Christ? Are you ready to make an impact, right in the place where you live? Are you ready to reach the world by reaching ONE?

Chapter One

Send Out the Workers!

The Storms of Life
Cindy

It was the day the evacuees from Hurricane Katrina first began to arrive at our church. As I drove up, I remember thinking it was chaos—organized chaos, but still chaos. There were people everywhere, both adults and children, evacuees fresh from the trauma of the hurricane and church members eager to help. Some volunteers were bringing in cots and bedding, while others looked for ways to help the evacuees. Luggage of all shapes and sizes—whatever the people from New Orleans had been able to bring—was carried, held, or stacked in piles. Cars, trucks, vans, and buses filled the driveway and the street.

Once inside, I saw that the gymnasium was filled with families trying to set up some semblance of a space of their own, a refuge in the midst of tragedy—a sanctuary in every sense. Adults, desperate for any scrap of information about the homes or the families they were forced to leave behind, were trying to find a television so that they could hear the latest news from New Orleans. The church office area was turned into a place for check-in and checkout, where needs were determined and decisions were made for how a person or a family could be helped. There were physical, emotional, financial, and, of course, spiritual needs. Our church had become a rescue site.

We served over five hundred people—as many as we could fit in the church and many more in homes across the area. Most of those who stayed in volunteers' homes still ate meals at the church and came to visit during the day. We fit as many beds and cots in the gym as it would hold, and then we filled up the small-group classrooms as well.

One of the biggest concerns was medical needs. We had to determine quickly if any evacuees were so ill that they needed to be isolated from the others. We took many people to doctors and hospitals, and thankfully, most of the doctors offered free services and medicine. Our church provided three meals a day and clothing as needed while other churches of a variety of denominations helped by donating food and clothes. We set up portable showers, and when more were needed, we arranged a schedule for taking evacuees to other churches and schools to use the showers there.

The needs were immense, and as the days passed, it soon became clear that the evacuees' stay would not be short-term. They needed help locating loved ones, finding new places to live, and obtaining work. During that time, we helped with all of those needs and everything in between.

One of the first things we did was to make televisions available so the evacuees could continue to be updated on the aftermath of the hurricane. They watched anxiously, soaking up everything they could find out about their homes, families, and community.

The children needed to be enrolled in daycares or schools. We did not have a full-time daycare, so we began searching for openings around town for the younger ones. The elementary children were easily placed in nearby schools, but the high school students were more difficult to place. I remember driving the youth and their parents to the schools to register, and I tried to see things through the eyes of these kids: They were taken from their homes with few or none of their possessions. Their parents were distracted with their own problems of providing for their children and deciding whether to make a home in a new place or try to wait and return to New Orleans. Some of these kids were away from their families and friends; others had lost them. They were hurt, confused, grieving, and unsure of their futures—and now they had to carry on with life in a new school. Small wonder that they looked so lost . . . it broke my heart.

Yet in the midst of that heartache and despair, God acted through his people in a mighty way. Our church members volunteered day and night, and more importantly, they ministered out of love day and night. We provided activities for the children and the adults. School buses were routed to pick up children at the church, and help was given to prepare parents as they went to interview for jobs. There were some great athletes affected by the storm who had been recruited by schools in areas around the city, and we made provisions to help get them where they needed to be. We tried to meet needs wherever we could.

Our guests were incorporated into our church activities and we treated them as family. In fact, our Wednesday night supper felt like an old-time reunion as the whole church joined together. We canceled many of our regular activities and added specific programs to assist the needs of the evacuees and their families. People at our church did so many extra things to help that I will never know them all.

It turned out to be an unforgettable, life-changing experience for all of us. We weren't just ministering to the evacuees; God was ministering to us. He was so real and close—we could feel him guiding us. Even though it was such a tragedy, Scotty and I both consider it one of the most important ministries of our lives. We learned more about who God is in that time than in any other. We learned how he works in the lives of people in times of intense fear and worry, and how, out of it, he brings peace and love. Some of the people of New Orleans stayed in West Monroe, have made homes there, and now continue their friendships with the members of the church.

God gave us a great opportunity to live out the command of "Love your neighbor," and when we allowed him to send us as workers into his fields, the result was a harvest of peace, joy, renewed commitment, friendship, and salvation.

Tragedies like Hurricane Katrina highlight the human need for connection, particularly in the darkest times—the God-placed need for comfort, peace, and relationship . . .

the need for Christ. As Christians, we know peace and joy in a way that is difficult to put into words. We know daily what it means to have a loving Father who has sent his Spirit to comfort us when we are hurting or afraid. So why are we not sharing this gift—God's love—with anyone who will listen? Why are we not shouting it from the rooftops?

The truth is, the lost and hurting are not just those coming out of a national disaster or a wide-scale tragedy. They are all around us. They are our neighbors, our in-laws, our servers at restaurants, our postal workers. They are our flight attendants or the people who bag our groceries at the supermarket or those who deposit our checks at the bank. They surround us.

> So why are we not sharing this gift—God's love—with anyone who will listen? Why are we not shouting it from the rooftops?

If we are to live as Christians—as Christ followers—we need to understand how Jesus views the lost. We need to know how he has asked us to show our love for him. The harvest is ready; we need to pick up our tools and start bringing it in.

The harvest is plentiful, but the workers are few.
Ask the Lord of the harvest, therefore, to send
out workers into his harvest field.
—Luke 10:2

Do You Love Me?

The harvest field is one of many metaphors that Jesus used when teaching about the importance of showing God's love to others. After Jesus was raised from the dead, he appeared to his disciples for the third time and had an interesting conversation with Simon Peter:

> When they had finished eating, Jesus said to Simon Peter, "Simon son of John, do you truly love me more than these?"
>
> "Yes, Lord," he said, "you know that I love you."
>
> Jesus said, "Feed my lambs."
>
> Again Jesus said, "Simon son of John, do you truly love me?"
>
> He answered, "Yes, Lord, you know that I love you."
>
> Jesus said, "Take care of my sheep."
>
> The third time he said to him, "Simon son of John, do you love me?
>
> Peter was hurt because Jesus asked him the third time, "Do you love me?" He said, "Lord, you know all things; you know that I love you."
>
> Jesus said, "Feed my sheep" (John 21:15–17.)

When you love someone, you want to serve that person. How do we serve Jesus? Feed his sheep! Jesus is not only instructing Peter, he is also teaching us through his Word. Simon Peter was good at boasting out loud of his love for Christ, but was he good at demonstrating his love in action? Jesus gives the point extra emphasis by asking his question three times. Although he knows the answer—and it frustrates Simon Peter—it should give all of us something to carefully consider: are we living out the love for others that Jesus modeled?

"Feed my lambs. . . . Take care of my sheep. . . . Feed my sheep." How do we accomplish these things? As Christians, we can take on the characteristics of a shepherd who will care for, guide, and spiritually nurture others to the safe arms of a Heavenly Father. Ministering to the hurting, showing compassion to the needy, and providing spiritual food from God's Word . . . all of these actions show Jesus' love. These should not be "things" we do, but rather *who we are*. We should not simply *do* love, but *be* love on a daily basis—God's hands and feet, allowing his love to change our very identities from the inside out.

This is how we know that we love the children
of God: by loving God and carrying out his commands.
This is love for God: to obey his commands. And
his commands are not burdensome.
—1 John 5:2–3

So if we have been given the greatest gift in all of history—the saving love of God through Christ Jesus—and God's greatest wish is for us to share that love with others, then what is stopping us? What is keeping us back? Why are we not feeding his sheep or working in his harvest fields?

It's Not My Responsibility— I'm Not a Pastor

It may surprise you to learn that one of the main reasons why people never share their faith is because they do not think it is their responsibility. One term we often hear from pastors is the word "revelation." For many people, both in and out of church, it comes as a revelation—an "enlightening or astonishing disclosure," according to Mr. Webster—that carrying out the Great Commission from God is not optional but a requirement for all Christ followers. This may explain why very few people in our churches are engaged in evangelism.

Imagine being one of the original disciples. Jesus had died and he had risen from the dead, but they were not sure what to do next. He came to the disciples once again to give them his last instructions. On a mountain in Galilee, Jesus appeared to his eleven disciples and gave them the Great Commission. It was not just for the original disciples, but also for *all who believe in Jesus*. There could be no doubt about who Jesus was because he claimed all authority in heaven and earth. Upon that authority, he commanded his disciples to carry out this mission to the world:

> *Then Jesus came to them and said, "All authority*
> *in heaven and on earth has been given to me.*
> *Therefore go and make disciples of all nations, baptizing*
> *them in the name of the Father and of the Son and of the*
> *Holy Spirit, and teaching them to obey everything*
> *I have commanded you. And surely I am with*
> *you always, to the very end of the age."*
> —Matthew 28:18–20

- "Go": reach out to others
- "Make disciples": evangelize, make new believers, and encourage spiritual growth

- **"Baptizing"**: help these followers identify with Jesus as a public profession of faith
- **"Teaching"**: lead people to grow in faith and personal relationship with Jesus

After Jesus shared what he wanted his disciples to do, he made them a promise: "And surely I am with you always, to the very end of the age." Even though he gave them a huge job, the disciples had hope because they knew Jesus would be there to help them. He commanded them to reach out to others, living a life of ministry and following his example.

What does the Great Commission mean for us today? It is interesting that the first command is "go." In the original Greek, the word "go" means "as you go." When Jesus spoke, he assumed that they would not be staying still, but would be *going*. Reaching out to others should not be a planned activity but should happen naturally as a part of our everyday lives.

"Making disciples" states what should be the top priority in the church's mission. "Baptizing" will come when those who have become disciples take the next step in publicly making a stand for Christ. The final command, "teaching," is the continuing task of the church. This process begins but never ends.

When we obey God by fulfilling the Great Commission and sharing his love with others, we grow in our relationship with him. By learning to give Jesus' love to others, you acquire more of him in your own life.

A Believer, But Not a Follower?

Some people hear of the Great Commission and think, *That command is for missionaries overseas.* However, Jesus calls *all* his followers to share the Good News of salvation throughout the world. His plan is for all believers to grow into disciples, following his commandments and example of evangelism. Mission fields can be across the world or very near home. There are people all around us who need Jesus Christ; often it is someone right next door. There are approximately two billion Christians in the world. What if each one were to reach one person for Christ, and then that person were to reach one more? As you can see, theoretically, if each one reached one in a year, there would be six billion Christians—approximately the world's population.

> Christ sends us into the world so that others, in seeing our lives, would see him.

Sadly, many adults cannot correctly identify the Great Commission as the commandment of Christ to tell the world his story and therefore do not have a clue what it means. We are losing ground, partly because we focus on the wrong things in church most of the time. Jesus never intended the Great Commission to be so complicated—*we* have made it that way. It is meant to be ONE reaching ONE reaching ONE. . . .

Let us quit playing church and be the church God intended. Are you ready?

Christ in Me

I have been crucified in Christ,
and I no longer live, but Christ lives in me.
—Galatians 2:20

Christ sends us into the world so that others, in seeing our lives, would see him. We are his ambassadors—his messengers to the world. In some ways, this is a scary thought. I think about all the cars I have seen with Christian stickers on them, loaded with people who are screaming or making gestures at cars around them. We are all sinners and make mistakes daily, and it is OK to let others know we are human. The important thing is to let them know we have a Savior who forgives and loves us anyway.

As witnesses, our primary function is to make known and manifest the life of Jesus. If we wait until we are perfect to share the love of Christ, we will never share. Are you worried because you feel too imperfect, too flawed to serve as God's ambassador? Consider Moses—when God called him to serve, his first reaction was to make excuses.

Moses felt inferior and ill-equipped to serve God. He told God that he had a speech impediment and was not equipped to direct people or lead others. God promised to supply the help Moses felt he needed, telling Moses that he could use his brother Aaron for the speeches that God would ask him to deliver. God covered all of Moses' excuses and needs. But you know, I don't recall one time that Moses was caught speechless and was unable to clearly relate God's plans and instructions. Even though Aaron was there and available, God raised up Moses to the task he had asked of him, and God used Moses to deliver the Israelites from hundreds of years of slavery in Egypt.

God will supply your every need, but with God, needs often disappear—what you felt was lacking, you find God placed within you all along. Take heart—a flawed Christian sharing Christ is all that is needed. Trust in God for a good outcome. He specializes in using the most unlikely of candidates.

The Greatness of the Commission

There are several things that are really "great" about the Great Commission:

- We don't have to come up with anything original—we simply deliver the message of God.
- We are being sent by God and he will enable us every step of the way.
- We don't have to be alone; the Holy Spirit is with us.
  - ○ "Never will I leave you; never will I forsake you. So we say with confidence, the Lord is my helper; I will not be afraid. What can man do to me?" (Heb. 13:5–6).
- We will receive power to represent Christ.
  - ○ "But you will receive power when the Holy Spirit comes on you; and you will be my witnesses in Jerusalem, and in all Judea and Samaria, and to the ends of the earth" (Acts 1:8).

Isaiah's Commission

Would it be easier if we received a commission from God the way Isaiah did? To paraphrase, Isaiah saw the Lord seated on a throne in the temple with seraphs (angels) above him. The seraphs were calling to one another, "Holy, holy, holy is the Lord Almighty; the whole earth is full of his glory" (Isa. 6:3).

At the sound of the angels' voices, everything began to shake and the temple was filled with smoke. Isaiah was struck with terror and cried out, "Woe to me! . . . I am ruined! For I am a man of unclean lips, and I live among a people of unclean lips, and my eyes have seen the King, the Lord Almighty" (Isa. 6:5). One of the seraphs then touched his mouth with a hot coal and spoke to him these words: "Your guilt is taken away and your sin atoned for" (Isa. 6:7).

Believe it or not, the story gets better—Isaiah actually hears the voice of God! Isaiah writes in verse 8: "Then I hear the voice of the Lord saying, 'Whom shall I send? And who will go for us?' And I said, 'Here am I. Send me!'"

Consider this situation for a moment. If this had happened to you and God asked, "Whom shall I send?" how would you have responded? Would you have said, "Well, I really have a lot to do this week," or "I get really nervous when I talk to strangers" (remember Moses)? If you think of it this way, then any and all excuses seem "lame," as the teenagers used to say. What excuses would come to your mind if God asked for volunteers this very moment? Are you ready to let go of your excuses and grab onto God's commission?

Go, make disciples, baptize—it is God's plan.

The Need

Following the attacks of 9/11, there was a noticeable spike in church attendance as people found themselves in a desperate situation and a questionable time. Many church leaders expected to see an intense spiritual reaction to the terrorist attacks and prayed that the new interest would continue. The sad fact that there was no lasting impact from the most significant act of war against our country on our own soil says something about the spiritual complacency of the American public.

Statisticians say that 89 percent of churches in the US are not experiencing healthy growth, which is another way of saying church attendance is on a definite decline. The integrity of the average American has drastically dropped and continues to deteriorate. This is why we must take a bolder, greater initiative in affecting our community.

This book is designed to inspire, equip, and challenge you to commit the next twelve months to showing one unsaved or unchurched individual the love of God. In one sense, this is a small request. Surely each of us can commit to being a continually faithful, Christ-like friend to another person who needs to meet Jesus. However, this is a God-sized goal when you look at the statistics in the average church, taken from the Barna Group's website and the books *Retreat or Risk: A Call for a Great Commission Resurgence* and *Unbinding the Gospel:*

- Less than 12 percent of church attendees share Christ each year.
- It takes fifty-three church members to reach one lost individual.

- Only 2 percent of church members are committed to building the Kingdom of God.

God Sends a Word

One day during my time with the Lord praying and reading Scripture, I felt an urgent word from him about a particular passage. On that day, God burned Luke 10:2 into my heart and mind: "The harvest is plentiful, but the workers are few. Ask the Lord of the harvest, therefore, to send out workers into his harvest field."

When I read that verse, I knew my calling with ONE Focus was to help pastors gather more workers into the harvest. A few weeks later, I had the opportunity to meet with the pastor of First West, Dr. John Avant.

"Scotty," John told me, "God has impressed a passage on my heart to share with you: Luke chapter 10, verse 2."

God had sent my first confirmation.

A second confirmation came recently when I was on a flight from Nashville to Dallas. My seat assignment was a middle seat, the least favorite spot of travelers everywhere, so when I arrived at the gate I requested an aisle or window seat. The nice lady behind the desk checked her computer.

"There's only one seat available of either type, and it's in the very back of the plane," she said. "It's very loud, and there's not any view."

"That's fine," I told her. "I'm planning on reading my book anyway."

As I maneuvered to the back of the plane upon boarding, I noticed there was a gentleman sitting in the window seat with a large cowboy hat on. *This should be fun!* I thought. I introduced myself and told him I had upgraded to this seat.

"I had a middle seat, too, and asked to be moved," he replied. (God's intervention, I think.)

The man's name was Donnie, and as I asked him a few questions, I found out that he lived in Canada. He was a missionary with the North American Mission Board, and he worked with Native Americans in the US and First Nations in Canada. What were the chances? Donnie was in Nashville because his father had just passed away. I believe I was able to encourage and minister to him as well.

Now, here is the cool thing that happened: At 10:02 a.m., Donnie's watch alarm went off. "The alarm is a reminder to pray," he said. "The 10:02 time is for Luke 10:2—to pray to the Lord of the harvest to send out workers to the harvest."

Another confirmation from God for me to stay the course!

We are now asking everyone who is a part of ONE Focus to pray at 10:02, either in the morning or at night. Also, as of the writing of this book, I am in dialogue with Donnie about rewriting our ONE Focus material to minister to Native Americans all over the US and First Nations in Canada. God orders our steps!

The Harvest

In Webster's dictionary, the definition of the verb "harvest" is "to gather in." We must reach out and "gather in" the people with whom we come into contact daily—*those with an emptiness that only Jesus can fill.* It is not our responsibility to save someone from sin, but it is definitely our responsibility to share the love of Jesus. As they experience Christ's love through us, the Holy Spirit takes over and does the saving part!

Unfortunately, as Jesus observed, the workers are few. Statistics from the three sources previously mentioned list concerns in these areas:

Evangelism

- 98 percent of Christians have never led one person to Christ.
- Only 35 percent of believers feel it is their responsibility to share their faith.
- Less than 12 percent share Christ once a year.
- Less than 0.1 percent (that's less than 1/10 of 1 percent) share Christ regularly.

Attendance

- 53 percent of Americans are not in church on any given weekend.
- From 1991–2004, the US population grew 15 percent. The number of unchurched adults grew 92 percent.
- 89 percent of churches are experiencing a decline in healthy growth.

Faith

- Only 18 percent of people surveyed said that completely understanding and carrying out the principles of their faith was their highest priority.
- Baptism in the United States is at its lowest level in twelve years.

These statistics state the problem before us. Things cannot continue as usual. Tradition and comfort cannot outweigh salvation and eternity. We must change and follow the simple and clear example Christ demonstrated in his mission and ministry on earth.

Jesus spent most of his time *showing* us what we would need to do. He was the master originator of "show and tell." It is his plan and example that ONE Focus follows. It is his plan that you are encouraged to emulate through ONE Focus living.

The Importance of ONE

The following is an excerpt from an article by Lillian Kwon on www.ChristianPost.com.

Half of pastors would leave the ministry tomorrow if they could. Seventy percent are fighting depression and ninety percent can't cope with the challenge of ministry. Those are the statistics Pastor Jonathan Falwell laid out to thousands of ministers who were in Lynchburg, Va., Tuesday for the "Refuel" conference.

Part of the problem, he indicated, is trying to make it to the big numbers and most influential lists or aiming for the most Twitter followers. "I believe that we have self-imposed measurements of success that are skewed, that are wrong," said Falwell, pastor of Thomas Road Baptist Church— which is notably one of the largest churches in the country. "The measurements of success are all messed up," he said.

While there is nothing wrong with the "Top 25" or "Top 100" largest churches or most influential lists, trying to make it to those lists has forced many pastors to focus on the masses rather than "the one."

"Stop focusing on the 'big ministry' and the 'big outreach,'" he urged, noting that ministers place too much pressure on themselves. "Start focusing on one person, one hurting person, who's lost . . . who's desperate to hear the Gospel." . . .

He reminded pastors on Tuesday, "We have a responsibility to minister to the one." And when pastors are faithful in focusing on one person at a time, Falwell believes God will then fill their churches with lots of "ones." So he encouraged them, "Don't make it about the lists, the fame . . . the respect. Make it about the one."

This is where you can help. God never intended for pastors to carry the sole responsibility of spreading the Gospel. Apathy in the church—in its membership—is a major contributing factor to pastors leaving the ministry. The task is overwhelming, and it cannot be done without the strategic mobilization of every confessing Christian. Some reports suggest that 15 percent or less of Christians are actually practicing what they profess to believe. Christians are generally living for the self and not for Christ. Will you commit to follow Christ's example and let him show his love through you?

This Is Love

At one church soon after the ONE Focus Initiative was first underway, a man who had committed to take part was killed in a car accident. On the front seat of his truck was found a list of the unsaved people he wanted to reach with God's love. The man's friends took the list and began praying for the names on it. One of the names was the man's father . . . who has since fulfilled his son's wish by giving his heart and life to Jesus Christ. Another accepted Christ on the day of the man's death when he heard of the accident and an explanation of the list his friend carried.

> God can use anyone—even you, even me—to fulfill the calling he has placed on all of our lives.

God can bring triumph out of tragedy, and God can use anyone—even you, even me—to fulfill the calling he has placed on all of our lives. It is my hope that this book will encourage and equip you as you reach the world by reaching one.

*This is love: not that we loved God, but that
he loved us and sent his Son as an atoning sacrifice for
our sins. Dear friends, since God so loved us, we also ought
to love one another. No one has ever seen God; but
if we love one another, God lives in us and his
love is made complete in us.*
—1 John 4:10–12

ONE Focus Living—Real-Life Testimony
Ruthann

Hey, I wanted you to know that my ONE, Jessica, accepted Christ today in Camille's Cafe. She grew up in Tulsa but didn't know anything about the Bible or Christ. She is a great, professional person, but she just didn't know. I asked her to lunch about a month ago; we had a great visit and then I asked her where she was spiritually.

She started out by saying she had been to church a few times, but she just didn't understand what was going on and didn't feel comfortable. After talking with me, she said she really didn't know anything about the Bible or the whole Christian thing. She said, "I always thought I kind of missed out on all that."

I decided I should start at the beginning, that we should work our way through the Bible stories, which she said she would love to do. We did Creation and the Fall of Man, but this week, they found out that her father-in-law has stage IV cancer, and it doesn't look promising. So today I told her I thought we should skip to the end of the story and then go back and fill in the blanks so they—Jessica and her father-in-law—would know about eternal life and how to find it.

She was very receptive and God's timing was perfect. It was a blessing.

Thanks for encouraging us with the ONE Focus emphasis. I'm looking forward to finishing the Bible stories with her. Now I will be looking for another ONE!

ONE Focus Challenge

There are four commitments you need to make. Approach these prayerfully, and then be prepared for God to move in your life as you say, "Here am I—send me!"

1. Commit to step out in faith
   - Will you reach the world by reaching ONE?
2. Commit to pray
   - Will you pray for yourself, for the ONE you are reaching out to, and for God's will to be done in your lives?
3. Commit to love
   - Will you be intentional and faithful in showing the love of Jesus to your ONE as you become a genuine friend?
4. Commit to equip yourself
   - Will you study the Bible, spend time with God, be involved in a local church, and feed your spiritual life with what you do, think, watch, read, and listen to?

None of these commitments should be taken lightly, yet none of the four are simply suggestions. They are requirements for the follower of Christ, and you can have faith that you will not be doing this alone. As you draw near to God and as you actively carry out his commission, he will prepare you for these tasks even as his Spirit guides you through them.

> Will you accept the challenge?

It's a dark world. Get ready to hold your light high.

Reflection

1. Do you feel the Lord pulling on your heart to help bring in the harvest? What do you sense that he is saying to you?

   _____

   _____

   _____

2. Do you feel ready to take a step of faith to reach others with the love of Christ? If not, what do you feel is holding you back?

   _____

   _____

   _____

   Pray that God would work specifically on this area in your heart and prepare you for the task that, as a Christian, he has called you to do—showing the world his love.

3. An accountability partner for *ONE Focus Living* is someone who will hold you accountable—and who you will hold accountable as well—not only as you study through this book together, but also as you live out its message. Do you know someone who could be your accountability partner?

   _____

   _____

   _____

CHAPTER TWO

An Unlikely One

To the Himalayas and Back

Scotty

In 2005 a good friend of mine named Ed approached me about going on an "extreme mission trip" to the Himalayan Mountains to reach a group of people in China who had never heard the Gospel. I prayed about it, and God did not tell me no. I had gone with Ed on mission trips to Honduras in the past, and they had been physically challenging—on the first trip, I had to ask one of the ladies if she could let me ride her mule for a while. At that point, all pride was gone! You should also understand that being a Boy Scout is not in my background. I really like a comfortable bed, hot shower, and indoor plumbing. Still, after my first trip into the mountains, I was hooked.

This trip into the Himalayas, though, would be much more rigorous than any I had been on before. It would require eight months of training. Nine of us would be making the journey together, and in a group of outdoorsmen, I was the odd one out. This is how I thought of the trip: how far am I willing to go to share the Good News of Jesus?

Randy, our leader, told us in our first meeting that we would have to hike four to five hours at a time with up to fifty pounds on our back at an altitude of twelve thousand feet. I had no idea what I had agreed to do! After buying my gear, it was time to start training. I worked my way up from walking with an empty backpack to filling it with a large landscape rock from our flower bed. I carried the rock in my backpack while I walked and, eventually, did the stair-climber at my gym. After only a few minutes on the stair-climber, I was very fatigued. My personal trainer, manager of the club, and good friend, Jim, stopped by and asked a question I will never forget: "So how much weight do you have in your backpack?"

I answered with, "I'm not sure, but it has to be close to fifty pounds." He suggested I weigh it on the scales and I agreed, wanting to show off my prowess. To my dismay, the scales said that rock weighed thirteen pounds. *Could this be some kind of joke? Could the scales be broken? This means I have thirty-seven pounds to go. This is impossible,* I thought.

However, God has a history of making the impossible possible, and sometimes it is in the places we feel the least prepared and most vulnerable that God does his greatest works through us. I did complete the training, and six months later, our team left for the Himalayas.

I left with a team of nine, including Dr. Michael Walker. Flying out of Monroe, Louisiana, it took thirty-three hours to arrive at our destination. It felt surreal to finally be in Kunming, China. When we arrived at the airport, we retrieved our luggage and I was assigned the bag with the religious materials that could land me in jail for a day or two.

"Go through last," Randy told me, "and whatever you do, do not let them put that bag through the X-ray machine." He must have seen the look on my face, because he added, "It's very unusual for them to run the bags through the X-ray, so don't worry."

All of the other guys got through security without any problems and were looking back at me. As I approached the security area, I was stopped by a Chinese officer with a rifle in hand. He said something in Chinese and I just ignored him and kept walking. He persisted and I tried to communicate with my body language that I did not understand him. He pointed his rifle at the bag and then at the X-ray machine.

I began to panic. All I could hear were Randy's words: "*Do not let them put that bag on the X-ray machine.*" My next step towards the door brought the rifle to my chest as if to say, "You are not leaving." My mind was reeling. *All this way,* I thought, *all this training, and I am going to a Chinese jail?*

As the bag was put on the conveyer belt, I could see my teammates' faces and knew it was bad. All I knew to do was pray that God would intervene. I was standing there with my head bowed, slowly walking to the exit, assuming they would tell me what to do next. When the bag went through with no problem, I picked it up and headed outside. *What just happened?*

The guys told me that as my bag was traveling through the X-ray machine, the person watching the screen was interrupted at the precise moment it passed. There is no question that God protected us. (Coincidences do not happen very often. If you are a Christ follower, God is working constantly in your life. Look for those glimpses each day of him working miracles. Instead of saying, "Guess what happened today," we should be saying, "Look at what God did in my life today!")

> If you are a Christ follower, God is working constantly in your life.

During the trip, which included a leech infestation and other things I will not mention, I became very ill. We were climbing straight up a mountain with no place to even stop and sit down. By noon, I began feeling very weak and nauseous. By one o'clock, I felt so ill it was the thought of dying that kept me alive! I was vomiting every few minutes and the team was becoming very concerned about my health. I do not think any of them wanted to explain to Cindy when they got home that I did not make it back.

This was my worst nightmare. I was so sick that I wanted to die, but there was no stopping in sight. The team discussed turning back, but I refused that option. It is not that I am a hero, but I could not fathom the mission being a failure. There was now an urgency to find a place to camp for the day. According to the GPS, we had at least another six or seven hours to our designated spot, but I could not imagine another ten minutes, much less hours.

Michael took point to lead the team up the mountains. Ed was behind me to balance every step. I will never forget

Ed's words: "Slow and steady." After each passing hour, I kept thinking I could not go on. Around five o'clock, I heard we still had two hours to go. I remember crying out to the Lord, "I cannot make it, I am done." Then it hit me. Part of my motivation for making this trip was the macho side of me. Yes, my pride put me in a desperate situation. I confessed to God, and within a few minutes, Michael said, "I found a large enough clearing that we can camp for the night."

The next day, we completed our mountain climb and reached the area inhabited by the Nosu people. We walked down the paths they often travel, placing cassette tapes of the Bible, sealed in plastic bags, along the weeded trails. We knew that eventually they would be found by the Nosu. It was pure joy to finally do what we trained and prayed to do—to drop off our precious packages of God's Word of Life. Since sharing Christ is illegal in China, we had to leave the packages and depart before they were located in order to avoid arrest.

Going down the mountain was much easier, and I was able to take in all the beauty around me. Obviously it took many hours to hike back, followed by the rides and flights home, but we accomplished our ONE Focus mission—to get the Gospel to the Nosu people of China.

An Unlikely One

That mission trip was definitely not the first time that I wondered whether I was up to the task. In 1986, after God got my attention with a burning building, I knew that he had better plans for me than the life I had been living. I even felt that God might be calling me to full-time ministry, yet

I questioned whether I had what it took. How could God use someone like me—a college dropout with no formal religious training?

Two years later, though, in the summer of 1988, Cindy and I threw caution to the wind and surrendered our lives to full-time ministry. We were both clear on God's calling, but we were far from certain as to what that would look like. You see, I still considered myself to be the most unlikely person for ministry at a church.

I had to learn that when God looks at us, he sees something different than what we see. He used all my past experiences to prepare me for my ministry, using me—as "unlikely" as I was—for his glory. The Bible is also full of people who were unlikely candidates, and God used them to accomplish great things. God used the life of each one to make a difference, and he can use your life to make a difference, too . . . no matter how unlikely it seems to you.

> When God looks at us, he sees something different than what we see.

The Story of Rahab, Joshua 2:1–24

It is approximately 1405 BC in the city of Jericho, in the land of Canaan. All of the city's inhabitants are overcome with fear of the Israelites, who have camped just beyond the Jordan River. The people of Jericho whisper to each other stories they have heard of how the God of the Israelites made a path through the Red Sea when they fled from Egypt, swallowing up their enemies, and of the utter destruction wrought by the Israelites on the two kingdoms of the Amorites east of the Jordan. They burn with fear and anger, and they turn to their pagan gods and idols for help—but none comes.

Two spies from the Israelites have entered Jericho in secret, coming to a house where travelers can obtain food and lodging, a place to enter and obtain information without causing suspicion. It is in a strategic location—high on the city wall, yet inconspicuous. The house belongs to a prostitute by the name of Rahab.

As night is falling, men sent by the king of Jericho bring this message to Rahab in Joshua 2:3: "Bring out the men who came to you and entered your house, because they have come to spy out the whole land."

Rahab's entire future, it seems, rests on the edge of a knife. She has a decision to make, one that could change her life—or end it. She knows that the spies are, at that very moment, on her roof where she has hidden them under stalks of flax, their lives in her hands. She draws a breath, perhaps whispers a prayer, and faces the men sent by the king.

"Yes, the men came to me, but I did not know where they had come from. At dusk, when it was time to close the city gate, the men left. I don't know which way they went. Go after them quickly. You may catch up with them," Rahab says in verses 4 and 5. So the men from the king set out in pursuit of the spies on the road that leads to the Jordan River, and the gate to the city is shut behind them.

Before the spies lie down for the night, Rahab goes to them in verses 9–12, her voice trembling but her eyes clear and determined. "I know that the Lord your God has given this land to you. . . . for the Lord your God is God in heaven above and on the earth below." She pauses, while the two spies look to each other in no small amount of surprise.

"Now then, please swear to me by the Lord that you will show kindness to my family, because I have shown kindness to you. . . . spare the lives of my father and mother, my brothers and sisters, and all who belong to them."

She waits, her heart pounding in her chest. She is a woman from a pagan background, a woman who has made her living through sin, the most unlikely of candidates, and yet—she recognizes the God of Israel as the Lord of heaven and earth. She has taken an incredible step of faith and placed her trust in that God.

"Our lives for your lives!" the Israelites respond in verse 14. "If you don't tell what we are doing, we will treat you kindly and faithfully when the Lord gives us the land."

And so it happened that Rahab saved the lives of herself and her family. After hiding the Israelites when the king heard that spies had entered his city, she helped them escape back across the Jordan River by lowering them with a rope out her window and over the wall. She risked her life to help the Israelites, and for their part, the spies were true to their promise. They gave Joshua a favorable report on the conditions in Jericho, and when the city fell, Rahab and all of her family were saved.

Despite her background, Rahab is considered a woman of great faith and she is held in high esteem in the Bible. The following passage was written about her centuries after her death: "Now faith is being sure of what we hope for and certain of what we do not see. By faith the prostitute Rahab, because she welcomed the spies, was not killed with those who were disobedient" (Heb. 11:1, 31).

Rahab had a choice to make. In choosing to serve God's plan, she chose not to be a part of the accepted "Jericho plan" of everyone around her—the consensus plan, the world's plan, the enemy's plan. I believe the spies went to her home because God wanted to save Rahab. She was a woman with a dark past to whom God gave a bright future.

The story doesn't end there, though. Rahab married an Israelite and bore him a son, and that son was Boaz, the husband of Ruth (another "unlikely" person of great faith). Boaz and Ruth were the great-grandparents of David, perhaps the unlikeliest of all—the bold youth who defeated the giant Goliath, the shepherd boy who became King of Israel. And David's descendant, twenty-eight generations later, was Jesus Christ.

Because of her choice, her willingness to be used by God in spite of what must have felt like an overwhelming unworthiness, she became an ancestor of Jesus Christ, the savior of mankind. What if she had accepted the lie, the lie that says "God can't use me"?

Do not let this lie take hold of you, no matter how unlikely you feel. Take a stand. Take a step. Take a leap of faith.

What, then, shall we say in response to this?
If God is for us, who can be against us?
—Romans 8:31

Today I am asking you to take your life and make a commitment to love one person throughout the next year. Each of us was created to love God and love people; this is God's prime direction for our lives. It is incredibly simple, yet for so many, so difficult to do.

Are you persuaded? If you have spent time in church or if you have read the Bible then you know God's plan. Are you going to follow his command and share his love with others? Every action begins with a decision. Will you be a spectator or an initiator, one who watches or one who gets involved in the life of one lost or unchurched individual? It is your choice.

> Will you be a spectator or an initiator, one who watches or one who gets involved?

The Body of Christ

If we know that God's will for us is to share his love with others, then why don't we do it? If we are dwelling in God's presence and understanding his heart for the lost, then why aren't we giving away what we have been given? The lyrics to the popular song "If We Are the Body" by the Christian group Casting Crowns highlight the problem by asking these questions of the church, the body of Christ:

If we are the body,
Why aren't His arms reaching?
Why aren't His hands healing?
Why aren't His words teaching?
And if we are the body,
Why aren't His feet going?
Why is His love not showing them there is a way?

If we are the body of Christ, why are we not living out his love every day? Why does it seem so hard?

Concerns over Sharing the Gospel

I am convinced that many Christians fail to show godly love to others because of concerns about evangelism. These concerns may even prevent them from beginning a godly, loving relationship with an unsaved or unchurched individual.

In a study of thirty thousand mainline churches taken from the book *Unbinding the Gospel* by Martha Grace Reese, people voiced the following concerns over sharing the Gospel with others. They are referred to as "Barriers to Sharing."

Barrier 1: Why?

The most consistent barrier of traditional evangelism is a lack of understanding about the need for it. If Christians do not understand the importance of evangelism, it is unlikely they will ever consider learning how to do it.

As we saw in chapter 1, the Great Commission was given to all Christians, and it is God's plan for his Church—not a building, a denomination, or one specific congregation, but the entire body of Christ—both then and now. It is a matter of life and death for the lost, and the outcome lasts for eternity.

Barrier 2: Fear

Traditional evangelism is seen by many people as confrontational. They view the act of sharing the Gospel with some prescribed evangelistic script the same way they view public speaking—with fear, dread, and a pre-determined mindset of "I can't, so I won't." They enter into it already believing they can't do it, and therefore they refuse to approach a stranger and address the lost life he or she may be living. They could have all the biblical knowledge and know-how in the world, but if they have this debilitating fear, they will not act. This fear *must* be addressed and overcome.

ONE Focus addresses this fear directly and teaches how sharing Christ can be a simple matter of living a Christ-like life. ONE is evangelism as Christ demonstrated it. He focused on a few ONEs called disciples and demonstrated what they needed to do in order to live rightly. We *can* and *must* do the same!

> ONE is evangelism as Christ demonstrated it.

Barrier 3: How?

A third common barrier to sharing the Gospel is ignorance of how to do so. Many admit, "I don't know how to talk about my faith."

ONE Focus is *demonstrational* evangelism. Yes, it may mean you share your personal testimony or the plan of salvation at some point in the relationship. However, it is not so much words as it is lifestyle, spiritual culture, and everyday life simply shown as an expression of Christ's love. It happens right where we live, with the people we see day in and day out.

So What's Your Excuse?

Cindy

Many times, I hear people say, "Everyone I know already attends church." I suppose in a small community that could be possible, but even in these communities, there are still people you should *get to know* who do not attend church or know about Jesus.

We pass so many men, women, boys, and girls each day without even really noticing them. The cashier at the gas station, the clerk at the grocery store, the child who plays on the corner . . . God loves each one of these and is waiting for someone to share his love with them.

Committing to ONE Focus may require you to get out of your comfort zone, but the rewards are eternal. My heart still races right before I start to share about Jesus. But as soon as I begin talking, the Holy Spirit seems to take over and speak for me. I have had many ONEs in the past few years and God has brought them to me in the everyday walk of life.

One couple I built a relationship with owned a nail shop. I ministered to them when they had their two children, helped them find a daycare, and bought their girls Christmas presents. They attended a church out of duty instead of a personal relationship with Jesus, so I talked about my walk with Jesus and what he did in my life each day. They visited our church for a couple of special events, so I am praying that seeds were planted. Since we have moved, I have not heard from them—they are in God's hands!

Another ONE was a waitress at IHOP where we frequently ate on Sunday nights. We would ask if she had any needs we could pray about while we prayed for the meal, and she would let us know the heartache she had in her family. After she shared with us, others would come and give us prayer requests as well. We became the ministers of

IHOP and it was incredible. We were able to share Jesus with so many people. Right before we left West Monroe to move to Texas, they had built a new IHOP and all the waiters and waitresses at our normal restaurant told us we could not go to the new one, we had to keep coming there. Sometimes if you find ONE, others will come, too!

Now, everywhere I go, I am always sensitive to God leading me to speak an encouraging word to someone. It might be ONE I will never see again, but at least I can say, "Jesus is my personal Lord and Savior and he wants you to know you are special and he loves you." It doesn't take much to bless someone and it might change a life forever!

Five Lessons from God

Ordinary people—people like you and me—can be used by God to accomplish great things for his kingdom. As you commit to ONE Focus and carrying out the Great Commission, you may feel excited, intimidated, overwhelmed, anxious, eager, scared, or all of the above. You may feel alone, like you are out there by yourself, or you may feel embarrassed, like you are doing something silly or socially inappropriate by approaching someone strictly out of God's love. It is important to remember not just that you are God's ambassador, but to remember the character of the God you represent. Here are five lessons that God taught me during the time surrounding Hurricane Katrina, when he did amazing things in our lives and in our church. He showed me that even the unlikely or the ordinary can be instruments in his hands.

Lesson One:
God Uses the Unexpected

*"For my thoughts are not your thoughts, neither are your
ways my ways," declares the Lord.*
—Isaiah 55:8

We have already seen how God uses the unlikeliest of
candidates to accomplish his purposes, but God also uses
unlikely and unexpected circumstances. We cannot always
understand nor predict how, when, or where God will move.

In 2005 Cindy and I were serving at First Baptist Church
of West Monroe, Louisiana, where I had been on the
ministerial staff for nineteen years. It was to be a year unlike
any other at First West; in a short amount of time, a number
of significant events happened that we did not expect. First
West's much-loved senior pastor departed, leaving many
in the congregation and community heartbroken. Then
Hurricane Katrina struck Louisiana; thousands fled the
coast with nowhere to go, and our church became a shelter
and source of help for meeting physical, emotional, and
spiritual needs for hundreds of people. Then a large State
Farm regional office shut down in our area, causing the loss
of over one thousand jobs. A Guide Plant closed down next,
laying off another thousand workers.

Around this same time, Cindy—who was serving as the
children's minister—was dealing with a diagnosis of central
vertigo, a constant feeling of unbalance and dizziness.
Marvin Smith, the personnel chairman, my mentor for
over fifteen years, and one of my closest friends, was in a

serious car accident, and I was visiting him in the hospital several times a week. We were making strategic decisions about how to lead the church during this transition period. Numerous members of the congregation were among those who had lost their jobs; many committed, faithful members transferred to other areas to find work. It was one unexpected event after another, and it seemed like the enemy was trying to keep down First West.

Lesson Two:
God Expects Leaders to Lead

Do you know that in a race all the runners run, but only one gets the prize? Run in such a way as to get the prize.
—1 Corinthians 9:24

During this interim period, I served as the lead pastor and the rest of the church looked to me for leadership. The loss of jobs was the talk of the town; church members were making their concerns known; staff members were considering moving on to other opportunities; and I felt like I had the weight of the world on my shoulders. At the end of my first official day as lead pastor, I held a meeting at my home with several key leaders and their spouses. I was weary; I felt ill and anxious. No one really knew what I would share, and there was a sense of uneasiness in the room as I began to talk.

I told them that I was overwhelmed and understood the gravity of the situation, yet I felt in my spirit that it would be the wrong approach to circle the wagons and wait for a new pastor. I felt God was leading us to take new ground aggressively—an unheard-of move in an interim period. That night, as a group of leaders, we committed to live out our faith by trusting our Sovereign God.

Lesson Three:
God Honors Humility and Desperation

If my people, who are called by my name, will humble themselves and pray and seek my face and turn from their wicked ways, then I will hear from heaven and will forgive their sin and will heal their land.
—2 Chronicles 7:14

We chose to believe that God had strategically placed us there "for such a time as this," just as Queen Esther was told before she went to visit the king (Esther 4:14). Everything was against us, challenges seemed insurmountable, and our best would not be good enough. So we all prayed what we later called "the desperation prayer"—a prayer born of humility and desperation. Our prayer was that God would do something so incredible that it would be unmistakably from him.

After the prayer, the atmosphere in the room was one of peace, unity, and clarity of vision. The desperation prayer became the catalyst that allowed our team to launch possibly the boldest initiative in the church's history, an outreach commitment that led the church to experience all-time highs during its interim period. God came through and I give him the credit, just as Joseph did when he told Pharaoh about interpreting his dreams: to paraphrase, "I cannot do it, *but God can*" (Gen. 41:16).

Lesson Four:
God Is Still in the Life-Changing Business

"I have come that they may have life, and have it to the full."
—John 10:10

Out of the church's new outreach initiative came record highs of giving, attendance, and commitment, including a giving increase of $640,000 in one year, the largest small-group attendance in one week in the history of the church (3,500 people), and more people saved and baptized than in any two-year period in the church's history—over 600 people. We were set up for failure, and people expected the church to have a huge decline, but it was just the opposite. Church members experienced strengthened faith and a sense of awe at what God was doing. There were so many volunteers that people were waiting to serve. God poured out his blessings and answered our desperation prayer.

> God poured out his blessings and answered our desperation prayer.

It would have been so much easier to do nothing. We could have "circled the wagons" and hung on until a new pastor came on board. However, God had strategically placed me to lead First West during that interim time, so I was going to lead! We did *not* circle the wagons or give ground to the enemy. Instead, we *took* ground.

God is still in the life-changing business!

Lesson Five:
Jesus Came to Start a Movement, Not an Institution

Those who accepted his message were baptized, and about three thousand were added to their number that day.
—Acts 2:41

. . . praising God and enjoying the favor of all the people. And the Lord added to their number daily those who were being saved.
—Acts 2:47

It was during this time that God birthed the ONE Focus Initiative. When God gives a blessing, it is often something to be shared. ONE Focus began at First West as a gift from God, but we believe he intends it to be in churches around the world. ONE Focus has been successful in many churches and is gathering momentum to spread to thousands more.

Jesus did not come to found an institution—he came to start a movement. To be part of that movement, you don't have to be what the world would consider a hero, a leader, or a legend. You can be unlikely. You can be ordinary. And you can be used right where you are.

> When God gives a blessing, it is often something to be shared.

Not Always Easy

It's possible that the road to reaching your ONE with the love of Christ will be quite smooth and easy for you. It's also very possible that it will not. During my trip to China, there were many moments when it seemed that I could not go on, and you may face moments when you feel unprepared, rejected, worried, or even fearful that you misunderstood God's direction.

God knows our hearts, but he wants to hear our cry to him. Unburden yourself of your fears, confess any sins, and clear your heart of anything that is holding you back from experiencing all that God wants to give you. Trust that he has his hand on your life and that "he who began a good work in you will carry it on to completion" (Phil. 1:6).

Stay the course, keep looking for ways to show love to your ONE, and faithfully put your confidence in God's ability to use you as his instrument. God did not say it would always be easy, but he did say he would be with you always.

ONE Focus Challenge

Think about the talents, gifts, and experience that you possess, the unique qualities that no one else shares. Also consider your sphere of influence—who listens to you or looks up to you? You may not be a pastor, but you may be a father. God expects you to be a leader in your home. What is the spiritual condition of your household? Or perhaps you are a teacher, a manager, or a small-group leader. Who imitates your example or follows your lead?

Make a list of your strengths, abilities, and areas of influence. Then give it to God—thank him for these gifts, and pray that he would use them to accomplish his purposes.

Next, think about your weaknesses, fears, and insecurities—the parts of yourself you would rather not think about. Consider your darker side, the inner thoughts and worries that perhaps no one really knows except for you and God. Make a list summing up the biggest reasons and excuses you could provide that you are too unlikely, ordinary, or flawed to make a difference in the world. Then give it to God—ask forgiveness for any sin, and pray that he would be strong in your weakness. Realize that God has a reputation for turning ordinary Joes into kings and giant-killers.

Know that God is the giver of good things—including our talents—and also that he is greater than our brokenness, ordinariness, weakness, or failure. Give it all to God, and prepare for an answer to the question, "Can God use me?"

The answer, you will find, is a resounding *yes*.

Reflection

1. Literature, film, and popular culture are filled with "rags-to-riches" stories of ordinary people rising to accomplish extraordinary things. People love to cheer for the underdog, to see someone come from lowly beginnings to great heights. Do you identify with these stories? Do you see yourself as someone ordinary, waiting for that chance to accomplish something extraordinary?

   _____

   _____

   _____

2. The point of being used by God is not to achieve fame and glory by the world's standards, but to make a difference for his kingdom in the lives of his children. Are you willing to ask God to break your heart for the lost?

   _____

   _____

   _____

Chapter Three

As You Go

Living for Christ

Jason Cameron was a young man who loved God and others with a passion. The principal trombone player in the West Monroe High School band, he also loved to play the guitar and sing. Jason was easygoing and kindhearted, and it seemed he always had a smile for everyone he met. His quick wit and sense of humor put everybody around him at ease. He kept himself busy, including serving as secretary, vice president, and president elect of the Fellowship of Christian Students. He was also a member of the National Honor Society, as well as the band chaplain.

As a member of First West, Jason was active in the Axis Student Ministry. He took part in the LIFE Groups and Chi Alpha choir, and he ran the sound board during student worship. Jason was also involved with the media ministries of the church—he served behind the scenes, running the lighting and sound for the main worship services as well as special events held at the church, such as weddings.

Family was very important to Jason. He had special relationships not only with his immediate family, but also with all of his grandparents, uncles, aunts, and cousins. Jason never left his family without first giving a hug and speaking those ever-important words: "I love you."

Even with all his other commitments, Jason made it a priority to live his life as an example of Christ's love. He lived out his values daily and reached out in friendship to others he met. He was a good friend and loved to share his passion for Christ. He left for school with his little leather Bible rolled up in his back pocket, always prepared to share or minister to his friends. The comment most often heard when others speak of Jason is that he always had a smile and hug for you, no matter who you were or where he ran into you.

> Jason made it a priority to live his life as an example of Christ's love.

On June 30, 2005, Jason Paul Cameron went to his eternal reward. Around four in the afternoon on a clear, sunny Thursday afternoon, Jason and his girlfriend were en route to a volleyball game with friends from school and church. A speeding car on the other side of the interstate lost control, crossed the median, and hit their vehicle head-on. Both Jason and his girlfriend were airlifted to a trauma center. His girlfriend survived, and with God's help, she is picking up the pieces of her young life. Jason died from severe injuries at the age of seventeen.

In his bedroom, Jason's parents found four questions that had been handed out by his Sunday school teacher. These questions became a memorable part of the service celebrating his life, and this daily evaluation is a good explanation of the kind of young man Jason was:

1. What did I do for Jesus today?
2. What did I do to contribute to my family today?
3. How would other people describe my attitude to-day?
4. Did I spend time with Jesus today?

The Jason Paul Cameron Foundation was established to honor the life Jason lived and the legacy he left. His passions were his love for God, love for his family, love for his church, and love for his friends. The foundation awards both educational and Christian camp scholarships to young people who share Jason's passion for making a difference in the world. This information about Jason comes from their website; please visit www.jpcfoundation.com to learn more about this exceptional young man and to download a copy of the Daily Evaluation card.

Jason's daily evaluation reveals priorities that are in line with God's will for us—not merely that we demonstrate God's love for others, but that this love flow from a deep and personal relationship with Jesus. We must not simply be ambassadors for Jesus—we must also spend time with him. We must give him our whole hearts, and we must live out his love through our daily actions—wherever we go, whatever we do.

As You Go

I pointed out in chapter 1 that the original Greek for the word "go" in the Great Commission means "as you go." Jesus assumed that his disciples would be going—they would be reaching out to those around them. It would be a natural, ongoing process, not a one-time or occasional act but a daily way of life. When we are in close relationship with Jesus, in submission to God's will and guiding Spirit, then a desire to carry out acts of love and sacrifice "as we go" will result. Once you are looking for people to touch with God's love, you will find they are all around you.

When God called Cindy and me into full-time Christian service, both our children were young. Jenny was seven years old and Jake was four. You hear many stories about kids who do not enjoy being a "PK"—a pastor's kid—but our children thrived under the love and encouragement of a great church family.

Jenny and Jake lived the life of "as you go" ministry. They had no choice; it was just what we did as a family. Each Saturday, we helped in a neighborhood ministry that served boys and girls of other races. When we took meals to someone who was sick, they went with us. They accompanied us on visits to the hospitals and to welcome new members. Both children learned how to share their faith in Jesus at an early age. One night on an evangelistic visitation, Jenny's team won sixteen people to Christ! For his senior trip, Jake went on a mission trip to Honduras with Team Impact and helped with a crusade. Countless men, women, boys, and girls were saved.

Of course our children are not perfect, but both have given their lives to Christ and many things they did as children have taught them life lessons. For instance, because of the neighborhood ministry, they have no prejudices and are good friends with people of other races and nationalities. Having ministered to people in crisis situations and experienced other people's grief, sickness, and extreme need, they each have a very compassionate and generous spirit.

We always told the kids "our family" was in the ministry. One thing they would always talk about is that they would never be caught off guard or surprised if we started sharing the Gospel or praying over someone right in the restaurant, store, or wherever we were. To this day, they both have such compassion for others. Jake has a habit of "loaning" too much of his money away to the people that work for him or to someone on the street. Jenny has a mission field at her work, too, as she donates clothes, gives baby showers, or strives to provide whatever is needed. The "as you go" life is definitely passed on from generation to generation, as God promises in his Word:

> I will open my mouth in parables, I will utter hidden things, things from of old—what we have heard and known, what our fathers have told us. We will not hide them from their children; we will tell the next generation the praiseworthy deeds of the Lord, his power, and the wonders he has done. . . . so the next generation would know them, even the children yet to be born, and they in turn would tell their children. Then they would put their trust in God and would not forget his deeds but would keep his commands (Ps. 78: 2-4, 6-7).

Today, Jenny and Jake are both married with two children each, and they are now ready to teach those life lessons to their own kids. We pray they will choose to live "as you go" lives, which is my prayer for you as well!

As You Go— Real-Life Testimony
Jenny

The "as you go" life of ministering prepared me for situations that I would deal with later in life. Fresh out of college, I worked with children with learning disabilities and was able to encourage and love them for who they were. Later, God called me to be a voice for children in the foster care system as a court appointed special advocate. After Hurricane Katrina, our community was a place of refuge for so many people escaping the devastation. My job was to speak for the children who were abused physically and sexually. It was not an easy job, but I had been shown my whole life how to love others the best I could. God had called me to love his people—not just the easy ones, but also the ones who were different, hurt, broken, or poor. As I go forward, I minister to people because it is what comes naturally; it is what I have seen my whole life.

As You Go: Two Parts
There are two parts to any successful "as you go" ministry lifestyle. The first is loving God. The second is loving others. In fact, Jesus said that all of the laws and the prophecies were wrapped up in these two commandments: "'Love the Lord

your God with all your heart and with all your soul and with all your strength and with all your mind'; and, 'Love your neighbor as yourself'" (Luke 10:27).

Part One: A Love Relationship

God wants his children to enter into a love relationship with him. If you love someone, you spend time with that person—you have a growing, personal relationship. Spending time in prayer, Bible study, and quiet time with God demonstrates your love. If you do not have a regularly scheduled quiet time, begin *today*. God's Word is alive and active, demonstrating the power to move someone from the depths of despair to the heights of peace and joy.

Even though there are thousands of devotional books available, the most important thing one can do is pray, read Scripture, and then *listen*. Using a journal to record thoughts is also a helpful way to keep the communication going. A good way to study is to research a topic and read verses pertaining to that subject. Another great idea is to read a proverb or a psalm each day. You will soon look forward to the time and not want to miss it—God has much he wants to share with you personally. True religion is an experience of the heart that carries us closer into a living, loving relationship with God.

Falling in Love with Jesus

When we consider the first two commandments, our attention automatically dwells on the first: complete love toward God. He is our Creator, our Savior, the One we pray to, and the One who forgives our sins. If you do not have a growing love relationship with Jesus—one nurtured by time, commitment, and devotion—you are missing out on his greatest gift.

In Scripture, when God wants to emphasize something, he repeats it. We have been told if God states it once it is important, if twice it is very important. If four times—as with the phrase that we are to "love the Lord our God with all our heart"—it must surely be significant.

> *Love the Lord with all your heart and with all*
> *your soul and with all your strength.*
> —Deuteronomy 6:5

> *Jesus replied, "Love the Lord your God with all your heart*
> *and with all your soul and with all your mind."*
> —Matthew 22:37

> *He answered, "Love the Lord your God with all your heart*
> *and with all your soul and with all your strength and with*
> *all your mind," and "love your neighbor as yourself."*
> —Luke 10:27

> *Love the Lord your God with all your heart and with all*
> *your soul and with all your mind and with all your strength.*
> —Mark 12:30

The ABCDs of Loving Jesus

    A: **All** of yourself—what part of yourself do you hold back?

    B: **Build** a relationship—is there a strong relationship with two-way communication?

C: Commit your life—have you given your past, present, and future to Jesus?

D: Daily make a decision to serve—do you ask for opportunities?

What are the things that stand between you and your love for Jesus? Don't skip right over this part! The reason it is called ABCDs is because it is *basic.* Take some time to think about each area. Your relationship with Jesus must be right before you can be the tool he wants you to be for him!

Part Two: Love One Another

God repeated the verse "Love the Lord your God" four times to help us understand its importance. Do you know how many times he told us to love our neighbor?

Do not seek revenge or bear a grudge against one of your people, but love your neighbor *as yourself. I am the Lord.*
—Leviticus 19:18

You have heard that it was said,
"Love your neighbor *and hate your enemy.*"
—Matthew 5:43

Honor your father and mother,
and "love your neighbor *as yourself.*"
—Matthew 19:19

And the second is like it:
"Love your neighbor *as yourself.*"
—Matthew 22:39

The second is this: "Love your neighbor as yourself."
There is no commandment greater than these.
—Mark 12:31

The commandments "Do not commit adultery," "Do not
murder," "Do not steal," "Do not covet," and whatever other
commandment there may be, are summed up in this one
rule: "Love your neighbor as yourself."
—Romans 13:9

The entire law is summed up in a single command:
"Love your neighbor as yourself."
—Galatians 5:14

If you really keep the royal law found in Scripture,
"Love your neighbor as yourself," you are doing right.
—James 2:8

Clearly, God wants you to love your neighbor (who could be anyone you come into contact with, or could, of course, live right next door). Sometimes this is more difficult than we might think. What type of love is God saying we must have? We must set our minds to respect and serve our neighbor with love and faithfulness, showing favor and good will—regardless of circumstance. People can sense genuine concern, so be authentic in your compassion. Step out of your comfort zone and put love into action. Love is not a mental state—it is an action word.

> We know what Jesus would do; the question is, what would you do?

The story of the Good Samaritan is a great example of someone going above and beyond to show love in action. As you read the story, try to imagine yourself in a similar situation and answer this question: Would I have been too busy, apathetic, or afraid, and looked the other way, or would I have been a good neighbor? We know what Jesus would do; the question is, what would you do?

Before telling the story of the Good Samaritan, Jesus had been asked the question, "Who is my neighbor?" In reply, Jesus told this parable:

> A man was going down from Jerusalem to Jericho, when he fell into the hands of robbers. They stripped him of his clothes, beat him, and went away, leaving him half dead. A priest happened to be going down the same road, and when he saw the man, he passed by on the other side. So too, a Levite, when he came to the place and saw him, passed by on the other side. But a Samaritan, as he traveled, came where the man was; and when he saw him, he took pity on him. He went to him and bandaged his wounds, pouring on oil and wine. Then he put the man on his own donkey, took him to an inn and took care of him. The next day he took out two silver coins and gave them to the innkeeper. "Look after him," he said, "and when I return, I will reimburse you for any extra expense you may have"' (Luke 10:30-35).

Isn't it interesting that Jesus first said a priest passed by the injured man? Jesus told this story to a Jewish audience, who would have assumed that the injured man was a Jew. The priest was considered to be a representative of God, yet he passed by. The Levite would have been someone who assisted the priest, a spiritual person in a layman's position. The Levite also saw the man but did not stop to help. However, a Samaritan—who was despised by the Jews because of his heritage, due to a conflict between Jews and Samaritans dating back to the time of the Israelites' exile by Assyrians—had pity on the man and took care of him. The New King James translation says in verse 33 that the Samaritan "had compassion on him." The Greek meaning for compassion is "to be moved as to one's innards," which represented tender or emotional feelings. Even though we know in our gut the right actions, we often fail to act as Christians. The story Jesus told demonstrates that we are called to show God's love not only to our friends, but also to strangers and even enemies.

In verses 36–37, Jesus asks, "'Which of these three do you think was a neighbor to the man who fell into the hands of the robbers?' The expert in the law replied, 'The one who had mercy on him.' Jesus told him, 'Go and do likewise.'"

That is another "Go and do" from Jesus—he must really mean it! Living out your love for others shows a love for Christ. Jesus says to show compassion to our neighbor without any distinction of race, nationality, or religion. Are you neighborly? ONE man demonstrated to ONE individual the love of God. It is simply one loving one, and telling of that love by first showing it. Christianity is a demonstration belief, an action word.

On the night he was betrayed, Jesus gave his disciples a new commandment by which they would be set apart from the world. This commandment is referred to as Christ's law.

Love one another. As I have
loved you, so you must love one another.
—John 13:34

This is the distinguishing quality of discipleship: to love one another even through differences and diversity. Christ is one—his Church is one—but that doesn't mean everyone is the same. We are to celebrate each other's differences while we search for oneness in him.

Jesus showed us how to love and expects us to follow his example. We have a responsibility to demonstrate that love in our actions, not just our words.

This is how we know what love is: Jesus Christ laid
down his life for us. And we ought to lay down our lives for
our brothers. If anyone has material possessions and sees
a brother in need but has no pity on him, how can the love
of God be in him? Dear children, let us not love with
words or tongue but with actions and in truth.
—1 John 3:16–18

Love is a responsibility, with no parameters or qualifications. Just love one another!

Selfish—Who, Me?

There is something that can keep us from living the "as you go" lifestyle and doing what we should for others—it is called selfishness. Our culture teaches us to be focused on ourselves. Through the media we get the message that our wants and desires are the number one priority.

Almost all sinful actions can be traced back to a selfish motive. Selfishness is a trait we easily point out in others but deny in ourselves. What we do not realize is that love and selfishness are opposites—we cannot act out of real love and be selfish at the same time. Real love is self*less*.

> *Do nothing out of selfish ambition or vain conceit,*
> *but in humility consider others better than yourselves.*
> *Each of you should look not only to your own*
> *interests, but also to the interests of others.*
> —Philippians 2:3–4

Sometimes I can be so selfish with my own agenda. I am a very routine-driven person and must really work on adjusting my schedule to make room for those times God sends "divine appointments." I pray my business does not get in the way of serving and loving others.

God tells us to be others-centered, not self-centered. His plan is much better because it truly gives us fulfillment, while selfishness only leaves emptiness. As you begin ONE Focus, examine your heart and your motives, and be sure you are seeking to share God's love for the right reasons. Jesus had many critical things to say about those who perform seemingly generous, sacrificial acts for the wrong reasons, such as recognition or reward. If you find self-centeredness in your heart as you prepare to live an "as you go" life and find your ONE, now is the time to confess it to God, ask for forgiveness, and seek his will for you. God loves you and wants to use your heart, mind, soul, and strength—give it all to him!

Bearing Fruit

Remain in me, and I will remain in you.
No branch can bear fruit by itself; it must remain
in the vine. Neither can you bear fruit unless you remain
in me. I am the vine and you are the branches. If a man
remains in me and I in him, he will bear much fruit;
apart from me, you can do nothing.
—John 15: 4–5

When we know the one true God and his Son, Jesus Christ, we bear fruit. These verses from John are so powerful and perfect for ONE Focus; they are what the "as you go" life is all about.

My prayer is not for them alone. I pray also for those who will believe in me through their message, that all of them may be one, Father, just as you are in me and I am in you. May they also be in us so that the world may believe that you have sent me. I have given them the glory that you gave me, that they may be one as we are one: I in them and you in me. May they be brought to complete unity to let the world know that you sent me and have loved them even as you have loved me (John 17:20–23).

A critical part of ONE Focus is to have an ongoing relationship with Jesus Christ. As you love him, he will show you how to love others as you go. To show our love for God, we must love others as he loves them—no matter who they are or what they have done. That covers anyone you might meet, so be on the lookout in any situation.

Remember:
- Look at people through Jesus' eyes
- Listen with genuine concern
- Encourage others
- Meet basic needs before trying to establish a relationship
- Show love by action

I wish there were words to express the abundance of love Christ pours out upon us when we love others for him. You cannot "out-give" or "out-bless" God. Live the "as you go" life and find out for yourself!

The Little Things
Cindy

I want to share an experience that happened during Christmas. Scotty and I found out about a mom and dad who had three precious boys and weren't going to be able to buy them any Christmas presents. We decided to put one of those big tins of popcorn and some Christmas candy in a bag, and we also tied a Walmart gift card to the top so they could go shopping and buy gifts. When the mom saw the bag with the popcorn and candy inside, she was totally thrilled without even seeing the gift card. I thought, *How can you be excited about the popcorn and candy when you still don't have any gifts to give your children?* Needless to say, she was speechless when she found the gift card.

Ever since that day, I have tried to be excited about the little things. My grandchild's laughter, my husband's voice, my family's love, a call from a friend, the gentleness of a child, the newness of each day, the joy of feeling the presence of God in my life . . . the list goes on and on.

My prayer this year is that I will be thrilled about what is in the bag and then overwhelmed by what else God has in store. He *always* gives us abundantly more than all we hope for or imagine!

There are ONEs all around who need a touch from us. It does not have to be extravagant or even cost anything at all. An encouraging word or a compliment to lift their spirits might be all they need to help them get through the day. God wants us to see people through his eyes and have his heart of compassion. God wants us to be intentional in loving others, every single day.

ONE Focus Living—Real-Life Testimony
Christy

I just wanted to pass along a story about how God is working through ONE Focus. A few weeks ago in my small-group class for high school girls, a new girl, Courtney, started coming. She came with her friend Rachel, who is in a different grade and class. Well, this morning, one of my girls asked me how things were going with my ONE. I, in turn, asked her and the other girls how things were going with their ONEs. Courtney spoke up and told us that she was actually Rachel's ONE. After class ended, she stayed behind and asked some questions about giving her life to Christ. She shared that until Rachel invited her, she had not been in church since she was a baby because her family does not attend. She also shared that Rachel had encouraged her to begin reading Matthew, Luke, and John, which she had started doing. During this conversation, Courtney gave her life to Christ. Praise the Lord! These young ladies are sixteen years old and God is already using them to do great things for his kingdom! And it all started with ONE Focus! God is moving in our midst, and I just wanted to share this story to hopefully encourage us to remain persistent as we continue to focus on our ONEs—God is always working! And as you read this, please pray for Courtney in her new journey as a Christ follower. Pray that God continues to surround her with believers who will encourage her in her faith. Thanks for reading.

ONE Focus Challenge

The impact of "as you go" ministry comes from your willingness to be used by God in every circumstance, not only those planned in advance or part of official church activities. Think about the places you visit often, the people you see each week, and the needs of others that you encounter on a day-to-day basis. Make a commitment to begin showing love to those people starting today. Ask God to open your eyes and direct your steps, and then follow through on what he lays on your heart.

Reflection

1. The heart of the "as you go" ministry is Jesus Christ. Is anything standing between you and your relationship with Jesus?

    _____

    _____

    _____

2. Do you live your life in such a way that people who don't know you would realize you are a Christian?

    _____

    _____

    _____

Chapter Four

Out of the Boat

ONE at a Drive-Through

I like to pick up coffee on my way to the church office in the mornings, and for a while I was in the habit of stopping at a particular McDonald's each day. A young Hispanic man consistently took my order, and he was always smiling and very polite. I would tell him, "I hope you have a blessed day."

After a number of visits, I found out that his name was Ramon. I cannot explain exactly how God gives a burden for someone, but he does, and I felt this for Ramon. I looked forward to seeing him, telling him something encouraging, and usually giving him a nice tip. It was obvious that he spoke little English, but we were still able to communicate.

What confused me was this: if Ramon was my ONE, how would I be able to show Christ's love? I began to pray for him, but I had not initiated any spiritual conversations. I knew I was being hesitant.

One morning Ramon was not there. A few more days went by and he did not return. I was worried that God had provided a ONE, yet out of my hesitation, I had missed the opportunity to share about Christ. I asked another employee at McDonald's about Ramon and was told he no longer worked there. I was crushed! I felt certain that God had given me that assignment and I had failed.

It was close to the Christmas season, and I received an early present one morning. When I drove through for my coffee, guess whose smiling face I saw? Ramon told me he had just been filling in at another location for a few weeks. I did not waste any time and asked if I could come inside the next day and meet with him. Ramon agreed.

During the few minutes Ramon had for his break, I found out he was married and had four young children. He drove one hour to work each day. We did not get to talk very long, but our relationship was moving forward.

Since it was the Christmas season and we had a small group meeting in our home, we asked if any of the couples wanted to help us provide gifts for Ramon's family. I gathered the gifts and asked Ramon to meet me at my car during his break. Those kinds of moments are priceless. He was so thankful and was at a loss for words. He looked at me with a question in his eyes: "Why would you do this?" I told him Jesus loves him and God had placed him on my heart to show Jesus' love. I told him we would visit some more in a couple of weeks.

Finally, the time came when I was able to meet with Ramon and share that Jesus loves him and desires to forgive him of his sin if he will put his faith and trust in Jesus as Lord. That day Ramon gave his life to Jesus—another ONE for God's Kingdom!

Choosing Your ONE

Once you have prepared spiritually to begin ONE Focus, have begun living the "as you go" lifestyle, and are prayerfully seeking God's will for you, what next? How do you find your ONE?

The first step is to open your eyes and look around as you go about your daily life. Notice people and be sensitive to what is going on with them. It is easier than you think to find a ONE. Do not say, "I am never around anyone who doesn't go to church." That is just not true!

Look around the grocery store. The lady you see each week behind the deli may look downcast and tired. Begin a conversation and ask what time she had to come to work this morning. Sympathize with her about her working hours, ask about family, and so on. Introduce yourself and find out her name.

What about the parents at your child's football, soccer, or baseball games? Maybe you have noticed someone who looks like he or she could use a friend. Ask God to give you sensitivity in all situations.

People are all around us—in banks, restaurants, retail stores, libraries, post offices, and on and on—and they need Christ. Finding your ONE can be as easy as asking a question and then being a sincere, sensitive listener. You may be the only person who can reach them. Do not say no!

Strategies

For the Son of Man came to seek
and save that which was lost.
—Luke 19:10

- One of the items we recommend is the ONE Focus remembrance wrist bracelet to wear. It sparks curiosity and may prompt a spiritual conversation. The main function of the bracelet is to remind you to pray for your ONE (see our website on the List of Resources at the end of this book).
- Have your "people antennae" up; be looking for hurting and broken people.
- Always keep in mind that you start with the people you already know.
- Your workplace and home are your mission fields. Even if you work in a church—what about the building's service team, the landscaping team, and so on? (I have led nine different family members to the Lord, as well as several people who I work with.)

Dr. Michael Walker, the co-originator of ONE Focus and the Life Catalyst ONE Focus coordinator, related this story to me:

> During an interview with a pastor, I asked about his ONE. How had he come upon that person and who was it? After several moments of silence, he began to cry. It took several minutes before he was able to talk.
>
> "I am ashamed to say my ONE is a neighbor I have lived next door to for years. I never gave this neighbor's spiritual condition any thought until we began ONE Focus. I knew his name, saw him mowing his yard as I drove off to church on Sunday, but never asked him to join me. I realized

I was so busy with church that I had forgotten the purpose of church.

"God opened my eyes to the lost ONEs I pass by on my way to church each week. Now I know this may surprise you, but pastors are human and we mess up. I had failed my neighbor, but never again. My neighbor is not a believer yet, but I am working with God to change that."

It is a great success story when someone realizes he has missed the mark and takes immediate action to correct a spiritual wrong. Dr. Walker encouraged the pastor to share his story with his church. Showing flaws, weakness, and vulnerability helps others admit to and face those same limitations within themselves. It's OK to make mistakes, but it's not OK to continue when you realize the error—especially if that error is toward God and could possibly affect someone's opportunity to know Jesus and receive eternal life.

You Find What You Seek

Our minds tend to sort information based on our priorities. Because of the incredible amount of data our senses pick up—sights, sounds, smells—we only pay attention to the important things. For example, the human eye sees several hundred thousand images each micro moment, and it must process these images rapidly while focusing on one significant image within the thousands. This is simply a necessary skill. If we walked into a room and had to stop and notice every last detail before we could move on, we would never get anywhere.

Countless detectives in literature, TV, and film amaze their readers and viewers by their abilities to notice tiny details that others missed, from which the case is solved. They can step onto the scene and notice the one critical clue that dozens of others have walked right by without seeing. Real-life detectives, of course, have been highly trained to notice this type of information—the type that will help catch the criminal.

We all work this way, to one degree or another. Think about the last time you were searching for a new car. Suddenly, in a brand-new way, you noticed every car that passed. You noticed the color, the overall appearance, or how it handled. If you had already decided on a certain style and model, your senses were sharpened to each one of that type that came near.

Here is where I am going with this: what if we used that same kind of focus and energy in finding our ONE? What if you were constantly on the lookout for people to help, to bless, and to share God's love with? I think you will find that there are more opportunities than you would have imagined. Don't be one of the many who walk right by without even noticing. Be the one who sees and acts. We find what we seek, but first we must be searching.

Out of the Boat

If you have chosen your ONE, the next step is to approach your ONE and start a relationship—or strengthen it if you already have one. While it is a good idea to start with people you know, your ONE may be a stranger. Although some people might be comfortable starting a conversation with a complete stranger, others would sooner spend the afternoon getting a root canal. In either case, you must be prepared! Of the utmost importance is a strong foundation for your faith and a personal, growing, daily relationship with Jesus. To be successful showing God's love to others, you also need to prepare yourself to be God's instrument. This always involves some form of reaching out—and this can be a challenging thing for many people.

There are two important points to remember here. The first is that God has made you unique, and he has gifted you with specific talents, traits, and abilities in order to use you for his particular purpose. The second point is that while you have unique abilities that may or may not put you at ease ministering to others, God also expects you to get out of your comfort zone!

> God has made you unique, and he has gifted you with specific talents.

Jesus Walks on Water, Matthew 14:22–33

It is approximately AD 30, near the shore of the Sea of Galilee. The disciples have just witnessed a miracle. With only five loaves of bread and two fish, Jesus has just fed over five thousand people, with twelve basketfuls left over— one for each of the disciples, a reminder of the power and compassion of the God they serve.

Jesus has sent the disciples on ahead of him in their boat, while he goes up on a mountainside by himself to pray, demonstrating that even the Son of God needs time alone with the Father. As the disciples cross the sea, a fierce wind arises, and the boat is buffeted by heavy waves. During the fourth watch of the night, the disciples see someone walking toward them across the water in the midst of the storm, and they are terrified, crying out in their fear, "It's a ghost!"

Jesus immediately says to them: "Take courage! It is I. Do not be afraid."

And here steps up Peter. Peter the bold, the hot-headed, the impulsive. "Lord, if it's you," he shouts through the wind and waves, "tell me to come to you on the water."

Jesus responds with one word: "Come."

And here it is—Peter's moment of truth. One of many he will face. The boat is pitching in the waves, the wind is howling, the other disciples are staring in fear and awe, and there stands Jesus, waiting. What to do? Only one thing, that's what. He gets out of the boat. And he walks on the water toward Jesus.

There he is, and I can't imagine what is going through his mind as he feels the water boiling around him, the waves lashing, the boat rocking behind him, the rain pouring in sheets, the wind blasting, *and his feet carrying him across the water toward Jesus.* But Peter is human; the sight of the storm around him is too much, and he becomes afraid and begins to sink. His confidence turns to panic, and he cries out, "Lord, save me!"

Immediately, Jesus reaches out his hand and catches Peter. "You of little faith," he says, "why did you doubt?"

They climb into the boat, and the instant that Jesus is in the boat with the disciples, the wind dies down and the storm abates. Then the disciples worship him, saying, "Truly you are the Son of God."

Now, Peter sometimes gets a bad rap for sinking. He may have even felt like a failure for taking his eyes off Jesus, focusing on the storm, and letting his fear replace his faith. Yet the fact remains that out of the twelve, Peter was the only one who stepped out of the boat, in the midst of the storm, and followed the call of Christ when he said, "Come."

In the area of Galilee in Jesus' day, little children who misbehaved were threatened by their parents with the ghosts of dead sailors drowned in the Sea of Galilee, who supposedly walked upon its waters. Like our modern-day legends of the bogeyman, stories of these ghosts served as a warning. Imagine, then, the thoughts of the disciples when they saw in the midst of the wind and waves the figure of a man walking toward them on the water. It is no wonder that they feared it was a ghost! By stepping out in faith despite his fear, Peter helps us learn some important lessons:

- When the Lord calls, it is our responsibility to go to him. No delays. No excuses.
- You may be in the middle of a storm in life, with winds and waves stronger and higher than you can manage, but if you keep your eyes on Jesus, he will see you safely through the storm.
- Sometimes Jesus calls, and sometimes you need to volunteer. If you do, be prepared to hear him say, "Come." And then be ready to do the thing that may feel uncomfortable, unrealistic, or even impossible. Be ready to get out of the boat. With God's help, you may find yourself walking on the water, too.

> When the Lord calls, it is our responsibility to go to him. No delays. No excuses.

You know your level of comfort with social interaction, and you must approach ONE Focus with your personality and preferences in mind. If you are too shy in the beginning to start a conversation, perhaps you can leave a note of encouragement for someone. Whatever your comfort level, know that there are steps you can take and acts you can perform to show God's love to another. Also realize, though, that God is calling you to be his voice, hands, and feet—that voice cannot be silent, and those hands and feet must be on the go! Pray for God to give you the courage you need to step out of the boat, and when the time comes and you feel God urging you to take that step, don't hesitate. He'll be right there with you.

Planting the Seed

My wife and I have a habit of going to the same restaurants. There are several we like and we typically order the same meal each time we visit. The waiters and waitresses tend to know us and even know what we like to eat. It is almost embarrassing when we walk in and *they* tell *us* what we want!

Since we know the staff, we make friends and often find a ONE or a ONE finds us. At one particular restaurant, there was a young waiter named Sandy whom we really enjoyed talking with, and he became a good friend. We would always ask for him, and when we came in, he enjoyed treating us special. He would tell us what was going on in his life and we would try to encourage him. We talked to him about his spiritual condition and he would say he was OK. We wanted him to visit our church, but he would not give us a commitment.

After a few months, we moved to another state and lost touch with Sandy. A couple of years went by, but one Sunday, we were at our original church for a visit and Sandy came walking down the aisle to greet us. He said he was saved, baptized, and had been attending the church.

God works in wonderful ways and sometimes we do not even know the results. It is our responsibility to plant the seed—he will do the rest!

Approaching Your ONE

God is with you. You are his ambassador. You have been called to share his love "as you go"—not on special occasions, but as an integral part of the way you live your life, a living epistle, so that when others look at you they see the love of Christ. You have committed to sharing this love with one person over the next year. You have prayerfully considered this and have chosen your ONE. How, then, do you begin a relationship?

It can start as simply as asking someone how his or her day went, complimenting someone on a job well done, or thanking the person for their attention or service. It can be the smile on your face or the tone of your voice. It can be the tip you leave your server. (Christians should be the most generous tippers in the world! Doesn't it all belong to God anyway?)

It can be the little things. During the holidays, Cindy and I get personalized candy bar wrappers that say "God loves you and we do, too." We hand them out to people at the grocery store, restaurants, and others we see on a regular basis.

You can ask people about their family, work, or where they live. You can notice common interests: Does she wear a "Breast Cancer Awareness" pin and you just ran in the Race for the Cure? Does he work at the video rental store and you have a friend who makes independent films? Does she work at the bakery and you cannot for the life of you get your cake to rise? Does he drive that new electric car you've been looking into buying?

If it is someone you already know to some degree—an acquaintance, a friend, a neighbor, a relative—you can initiate a deeper level of relationship. Invite your ONE to a ball game, a movie, or out for coffee. Offer to keep the kids so he and his wife can go on a date. Ask her and her new fiancé to come over for game night. Tell about this great parade that your town is throwing for the holiday, and see if his family wants to come share some hot dogs and watermelon with yours.

The ways to approach a person out of kindness and sincerity are endless. Trust the nudging of the Spirit and act on it when it comes. Look for opportunities to show love not only to your ONE, but to everyone you come in contact with. Make a point to seek out your ONE specifically and make contact—step out of the boat and make it happen!

Here are more ideas for how to find or approach your ONE:

- When dining at a restaurant, ask your waiter or waitress for any prayer needs before you pray over your meal. In our experience, this has been a very touching way to reach out to others.

- Encourage people—where you shop, at the fast-food drive-in window, at the gas station, or at a ball park. Everyone needs encouragement, and the one who takes the time to smile and ask about someone else's day will become a welcomed friend.
- Use all of your senses to notice your surroundings. Listen to people. Are pictures of grandchildren displayed? What about a favorite sports team? Are people sad? Did they have a bad day? Connect to interests, find common ground, and relate to what is going on in their lives.
- If you have children, get involved in the lives of the parents by having a party for families.
- When someone new moves into the neighborhood, take cookies or a special treat basket.
- Coworkers and neighbors are all potential ONEs. Do their lives demonstrate Christ or a need for Christ? Do you know anything about them? In today's world, people are so busy that they pass by every day and never exchange a simple hello. Begin a conversation with someone you see daily. Let that person talk and be a good listener.

ONE Focus Living—Real-Life Testimony
Sarah

I have known my ONE for almost five years. We met at the gym. We have worked out together, participated in triathlons together, and have shared meals with one another. Since I've known my ONE, I've been aware that she doesn't have a personal relationship with Jesus Christ. In fact, she barely knows anything about him. She was raised in Germany, and her parents never took her to church.

I have tried to show my ONE through my words and actions that I personally know Christ. I have said things like, "I'll be praying for you," and, "What a beautiful day God has given us." I have even blessed her food and invited her to church. However, I have never actually told her about the love of Christ and what he did for the world on Calvary.

At the end of 2010, the Lord started working on my heart. The Holy Spirit began urging me to share the Good News with my ONE. Of course, as I sometimes do, I began reasoning with God by saying to him, "What if I offend her? Maybe I should wait until she asks me about you."

> First and most importantly, pray.

Then, in January 2011, I found out that my pastor would be asking the church congregation to participate in an initiative called ONE Focus. That is when I realized the Lord had been preparing me to tell my ONE about him for many weeks. Through ONE Focus, God has reassured me that he will give me the courage and words I need to reach my ONE.

ONE Focus Challenge

To find your ONE, carry out these steps:

1. First and most importantly, pray. Ask God to reveal your ONE to you, and begin praying for your ONE before you even know who it is.

2. Be sensitive to the Spirit. If you feel a "nudge" inside to choose someone as your ONE, don't question it—be obedient!

3. Make a list of the people you see on a regular basis—family, friends, acquaintances, coworkers, employees of businesses you frequent—then narrow this list to those who either do not know Jesus or you are not sure if they do.

4. Start looking at others with "ONE-focused" eyes. Watch for people who present opportunities to show God's love.

5. Trust God to guide you until your path crosses that of your ONE.

6. When you find your ONE, pray and prepare to step out of the boat—to approach your ONE and begin a loving, godly relationship.

Reflection

1. Are you willing to leave your comfort zone in order to reach the lost? If not, what is holding you back?

   _____

   _____

   _____

2. Do you have a family member you need to talk to about Christ? If so, what is keeping you from that conversation?

   _____

   _____

   _____

3. Have you found another person to partner and pray with as you work through *ONE Focus Living*?

   _____

   _____

   _____

CHAPTER FIVE

Closer Than a Brother

My Covering
Cindy

Scotty had been to Honduras a couple of times and had been so moved by the experience. I felt left out when he would talk about the people there, so when a trip came up that was not an "extreme trip," I thought, *This is my chance,* and we signed up to go. The week of the trip, Scotty and our son, Jake, left on Tuesday. I needed to remain in the US to complete some medical tests and would be traveling with a couple of other people on Thursday. Being by myself is not something I am used to, so God was already teaching me a lesson. God was also teaching Scotty patience, because he had to wait until I got to Honduras to hear that everything was OK.

Our time in Honduras was very short, but it was wonderful. The airport was a couple of hours away from where we were staying, so on a Saturday we left in a caravan to go back home. Jennifer, one of the missionaries, was driving with Scott (another staff member) in the front, and Scotty and I rode in the back of one vehicle, while Jake rode in the vehicle behind us. The roads were not very good and there were people everywhere. I was so afraid one of the children walking alongside the road would fall into the street—they walked so close. I also get very carsick, so I had to pray the whole time that I would be OK.

One moment, we were riding along safely, and the next, we were going around a curve too fast for Jennifer to keep control of the vehicle. We turned over two times and landed upright in a ditch. The peace that was in that car can only be explained by God. There was no screaming, only the sound of Jennifer saying, "Jesus, Jesus." When we stopped, Jake was at my window. Even though he had to watch it, he knows what I know—God worked a miracle right before his eyes.

Some facts that attest to God's hand on us that day:

- No one was hurt except for some scratches and bruises and Jennifer's sprained wrist.
- On every other place in the road there had been people walking, but no one was anywhere around us.
- Scotty had reached up and locked Scott's door a few minutes earlier.
- Everyone had a seatbelt on except Scotty, and Scotty used his body to shield me.
- Because of my history of heart irregularities, I faint easily. I did not faint or get carsick, even while turning over in the car!

- No other vehicle was coming as we flipped over or as Jake was running to get to us.
- We picked up the luggage, got everyone in other vehicles, and still got to the airport to get everyone home on time.

Why am I sharing this, and what did God say to me? I have always had someone to keep me safe and take care of me. Growing up in church, I have always had lots of people who tell me to slow down or say that I'm working too hard. Scotty, as wonderful as he is, could not have kept something from happening to me, no matter how hard he tried. Jake is a big boy and thinks he could protect his mom from anything, but he cannot always be there.

God was there with me. I felt his presence in such a way that it has given me new confidence in everything. I used to worry about accidents, things that might happen to my family, or the everyday issues of ministry. Now I can honestly say that I believe God has me here for a purpose and that he will keep me safe, he will protect me, and he will be my covering in all things.

I often look like I am on a mission, and I know I need to slow down, but

> He is depending on me to make a difference in this world, and he depends on you, too.

let me take this opportunity to tell you—I don't have it all together. I get discouraged and I worry about things that I shouldn't, but God is patiently teaching me to trust him completely. He is teaching me not to depend on others to make me feel safe and secure, because he is my best friend and will always be with me. He is depending on me to make a difference in this world, and he depends on you, too.

There is a friend who sticks closer than a brother.
—Proverbs 18:24

A True Friend

You have a name for your ONE. You have approached your ONE and initiated contact. Now develop your friendship and work to build a true relationship.

Jesus is the best friend anyone could ask for, and we should follow his example in our friendships with others. Be the kind of friend to your ONE that you would like to have as your friend. I believe Jesus said it this way: "Love your neighbor as yourself."

A few ideas to get you started:

- Ask your ONE over for a meal or dessert.
- Meet for lunch or coffee.
- In times of crisis, take a meal to your ONE's family, babysit, or help with other needs.
- Share a book, movie, or music that has made an impact on your life.
- Be a great listener. People need someone to simply listen. God gave us one mouth and two ears—use them in that ratio.
- Ask about their interests and hobbies. If you do not hear church mentioned, ask about their religious connections.

- Progress slowly and be patient. How long did God chase after you before you said yes?
- Eventually share your personal testimony.

These ideas have likely sparked others in your mind and heart. As you build those relationships, let the Holy Spirit lead you to share your testimony. Your personal testimony should be your strongest tool. You must take the initiative! Stepping out and developing relationships takes work. Ask God to give you insight and understanding for your ONE.

Serving Your ONE

Work hard to find the best way to communicate with your ONE. Schedule a weekly lunch, phone call, text, or online chat. If it seems comfortable, ask for his or her prayer needs. Celebrate birthdays, anniversaries, and holidays, and be there in times of crisis. When someone is in the hospital, take a meal. When someone dies, clean the house for the extra company that may be coming, take over paper goods, pick up the kids for them, or run errands. Instead of *saying,* "I'll pray for you," stop right where you are to pray with them immediately. Instead of asking, "Is there anything I can do?" tell them, "I am coming over to bring dinner tonight." Meet needs and serve with love. Do not get discouraged if there is not an instantaneous response or receptiveness, but patiently pursue.

Although Jesus was constantly being asked for things, he was a true servant. Maybe we could try following his example from these next two verses by just asking, "What can I do for you?" That question may bring your relationships to a new level! Love means serving others with true concern.

"What do you want me to do for you?" he asked.
—Mark 10:36

"What do you want me to do for you?"
Jesus asked him. The blind man said,
"Rabbi, I want to see."
—Mark 10:51

Picture Jesus washing the dirty feet of his disciples or offering compassion to the leper. Can you imagine serving in these ways? In today's world there are other ways to serve. One of the most effective is to freely undertake any commitment necessary to help with another's emotional or physical needs. However we choose to serve, it must reflect the character of Christ.

Who, being in very nature God, did not
consider equality with God something to be grasped, but
made himself nothing, taking on the very nature of a
servant, being made in human likeness.
—Philippians 2:6–7

What Does Your ONE Need?

After you choose your ONE, you must think about that person's needs. Every person has an emptiness within that can only be filled with God's love. Do we demonstrate what they are looking for? Do they see joy, happiness, and hope in us as we go through the everyday situations of life? The following verses must be true in our lives—shining light to a dark world!

In the same way, let your light shine before men, that they may see your good deeds and praise your Father in heaven.
—Matthew 5:16

For you were once in darkness, but now you are light in the Lord. Live as children of light.
—Ephesians 5:8

But if we walk in the light, as he is in the light, we have fellowship with one another, and the blood of Jesus, his Son, purifies us from all sin.
—1 John 1:7

"Shine," "that they may see," "live," "walk," "have fellowship"—these are all actions, not just words. Sharing Christ is not so much about moving your mouth as it is about letting Christ move your heart to touch another's.

How do you find out what your ONE needs? Get to know that person! Some people will open up readily and freely unburden themselves to the first person who will listen. Others will give their trust only over time. Learn their hopes, fears, dreams, and anxieties. Learn what they love to do or wish they could accomplish. Learn what they are passionate about, what makes them cry, what makes them angry, what matters to them, what keeps them awake at night—and then meet the needs as you can. When they ask you, "Why are you doing this?" (and they will), there is your opportunity—tell them you have been given the gift of God's love, and you want to share that gift.

In the early stages of developing a relationship, it may seem that it is moving slowly, and you may feel frustrated that things are not progressing faster, or you may even be overly eager to share the Gospel before your ONE's heart is prepared to receive it. Do not be discouraged, because God's timing is perfect. The seeds you are planting may even be someone else's responsibility to water, and another person's to harvest. Sometimes you don't know the impact you are making on a life. Be a faithful friend, and trust God for the rest.

> Sometimes you don't know the impact you are making on a life.

What Is a Friend?

A friend is:

- A person of discernment
- A person who doesn't expect us to be perfect in every way and doesn't hold it against us when those imperfections show themselves
- A person who knows how to laugh, how to handle tears, how to pray, how to be silent and listen, and how and when to offer counsel
- A person who can help us occasionally walk away from the intensity of life and discover all the fun there is in simply being someone who loves God
- A person who can be confidential and not judgmental, sharing each other's burdens only with God

Friendships take time! Are you willing to be the kind of person a friendship requires? Friends make each other better when they are together. The Old Testament friendship of Jonathan and David is described like this: "Jonathan went to David . . . and helped him find strength in God" (1 Sam 23:16). Jesus worked hard to develop a sense of community and friendship among his disciples. It's interesting to see how much Jesus wanted to be with his friends when he was troubled. He leaned on them even when he knew they would ultimately fail him in his darkest hour. He never became cynical or bitter but "loved them to the last" (John 13:1).

ONE Focus Living—Real-Life Testimony
Dr. Michael Walker

When my church began the ONE Focus Initiative, I began to pray that God would reveal to me the exact one he had chosen for me. I wanted so much for it to be God's choice and not mine. He was faithful and immediately brought an individual's image into my mind as I prayed. As this person's picture formed in my mind, I began to backtrack in my request. You see, the person God had chosen was not at all the person I would have chosen.

The person God showed me attended the health club where I worked out daily. I would see him every morning at the club and would greet him with a smile and a friendly hello as he walked by. Each morning, his response was the same: he would continue to walk by and act as though I had not spoken or even existed. He completely and consistently ignored me, my greeting, and my smile. In fact, he ignored everyone. He was the talk of the health club because of his unfriendliness, which most people interpreted as rudeness.

After a brief discussion with God and my attempt to get him to swap for a different ONE, I set myself up to meet the person God had chosen. At our next encounter in the hall of the health club, I stopped as my ONE approached, stuck out my hand, and said, "My name is Mike Walker, and yours is?" You can hardly ignore that! He gave me his name. Once I knew his name, I could greet him with it. As time passed I learned about his work, his family, and his beliefs. It was surprising how quickly he became friendly once I had gotten his name and made an effort to know him. I made a point to introduce him to others. It wasn't long before everyone in the club knew him and he knew them. Getting him to a realization of his need to meet Christ would take much longer.

A week after finding out his name, I invited him to join me on my morning walking routine following my weight workout. I was shocked when he agreed to go. Walking with someone several times each week provides much time to talk. We have had many discussions about our beliefs and about what the Bible says about salvation. We have even fished together and now play racquetball weekly. I try to

> God does not always give easy assignments.

show Christ to him as problems and difficulties come up in our discussions. He is a great guy, and he knows a lot about religion and much of what the Bible says. He just doesn't accept Christ's way as the only way to eternal salvation.

It has been over four years and he is still my ONE. God does not always give easy assignments, but since this ONE came from God, I know I will eventually succeed. I pray for my ONE to realize he is missing the best friend there is. We are not truly living until we live with God as our best companion, our dearest friend.

ONE Focus Challenge

Make a list of your ONE's most pressing needs, and then make a plan to meet or help with at least one of those needs this week. Continue to plan acts of selfless, Christ-like love for your ONE. Be a true friend—not the kind that is there only when it is easy or convenient, but the kind that sticks "closer than a brother."

Reflection

1. What is the nicest thing that you can remember a friend doing for you?

   _____

   _____

   _____

2. What made it so special?

   _____

   _____

   _____

3. Is there something you could do for your ONE that might touch him or her in a similar way?

   _____

   _____

   _____

CHAPTER SIX

The Heart Connection

Good Intentions

The other night, Cindy and I stopped at a grocery store on the way home from dinner. We pulled into the parking lot and noticed an older gentleman who was standing by his vehicle with the hood up.

"Maybe we can offer to help," Cindy said, noticing him first.

Even though I have limited expertise on car repair, I went ahead and asked the gentleman if I could help.

"I may just need a battery boost," he said.

I drove my car into position so we could connect the battery cables, and that is when things became interesting. First, I could not find the hood release to my car. Now, in my defense, I had only had this car a few months. Thankfully, the nice gentleman was able to locate it for me. Whew! I was at least able to pop the trunk without any assistance. As I frantically looked in the trunk for jumper cables, I made the stupid statement, "Doesn't every vehicle come with cables?"

The nice gentleman once again helped me out by saying, "No, they do not."

It became apparent that my good intentions were getting me nowhere. I did ask the gentleman if there was anything else I could do for him.

"Yes," he said. "Please move your car so someone else who can help me can park here."

Now, the point to this story is that we often go through life with good intentions, but then we are not equipped to really make a difference. Many times we cannot connect with others' hearts until we have served them in their place of need. Although sometimes your ONE will need help beyond what you can offer—you may not be an expert in car repair any more than I am—many times all your ONE needs is someone willing to make an investment of time and concern. As you get to know your ONE, you can also learn what your ONE needs and equip yourself to meet those needs.

There's a second, more important way you can equip yourself. You need to be equipped spiritually to make a difference in your ONE's life. After all, you cannot give what you do not have. Read God's Word, pray, and seek a relationship with him. Ask God to put others who you can minister to in your path. Be sensitive to his leading and the ONE or ONEs he sends your way.

Be equipped to make a heart connection, and your good intentions will have the right outcome!

The Heart Connection

Once you have begun a friendship with your ONE, be sensitive toward ways that you can deepen the relationship. This might mean meeting your ONE's family or inviting him or her to meet yours; it may mean trusting your ONE with vulnerable feelings or confidences; it may mean being a friend above and beyond the call of duty. This is hospitality, in the Christian sense—hospitality that looks a lot like serving others out of love.

When we minister to the needs of others, we open a possibility not for seeing eye to eye, but for connecting heart to heart. Jesus made heart connections everywhere he went. He didn't just speak love—he *showed* love by meeting needs and demonstrating that he cared. Although Jesus was the greatest teacher and debater the world has ever seen, he wasn't ultimately looking for a meeting of the minds. He was after a meeting of the hearts.

Christian Hospitality

Do not forget to entertain strangers, for by so doing some people have entertained angels without knowing it.
—Hebrews 13:2

This verse is framed and hung in our home as a reminder of the importance of Christian hospitality. Our children were brought up having guests in our home for fellowship. We even prayed over each room and asked God to bless our home and make it a haven for our family and others.

Hospitality opens the door for heart connections, but it does not always come easily. It takes effort and work. Consider the next three Bible verses:

Offer hospitality to one another without grumbling.
—1 Peter 4:9

Then Peter invited the men into the house to be his guests.
—Acts 10:23

. . . and is well known for her good deeds,
such as bringing up children, showing hospitality,
washing the feet of the saints, helping those in trouble
and devoting herself to all kinds of good deeds.
—1 Timothy 5:10

Hospitality is ranked with washing feet! (This is a good thing.) We must be willing to be the hands and feet of God, and that might include inviting and welcoming a guest into our homes. Remember that Christianity is best shared by demonstration—what we do is much more powerful than what we say. What could you do for your ONE that would reach your ONE's heart?

> What could you do for your ONE that would reach your ONE's heart?

Invite Your ONE

Has your relationship grown enough that you feel comfortable inviting your ONE to your home or to church? What about a fellowship event with some of your small group members, or a church-sponsored event that is less "threatening" than Sunday morning worship?

Just remember to meet needs. People cannot think about accepting Christ until their hearts are open to making that connection, and their hearts are often tightly guarded when they have immediate needs that are not being met.

> *For Christ's love compels us, because we are convinced that one died for all, and therefore all died. And he died for all, that those who live should no longer live for themselves but for him who died for them and was raised again.*
> —2 Corinthians 5:14–15

> *Therefore, if anyone is in Christ, he is a new creation; the old has gone, the new has come! All this is from God, who reconciled us to himself through Christ and gave us the ministry of reconciliation: that God was reconciling the world to himself in Christ, not counting men's sins against them. And he has committed to us the message of reconciliation.* We are therefore Christ's ambassadors, as though God were making his appeal through us. We implore you on Christ's behalf: Be reconciled to God.
> —2 Corinthians 5:17–20, emphasis added

On Christ's behalf, we are making an appeal to others. Our hearts are reaching out for theirs. If we don't reach out to them, who will? Because of John 10:10—"I have come that they may have life and have it to the full"—we invite. We have the greatest news that could ever be shared.

It will be worth the risk, and it could make a difference for eternity.

Jesus Invites Himself
Todd Parr

"Zacchaeus was a wee little man . . . and a wee little man was he. . . ." That is a very familiar tune sung to small children, yet if we listen carefully, we can hear a story of God's redemptive love and his possible plan for you.

Zacchaeus was a chief tax collector in Jericho. A small man, he was by no means popular. He had acquired his wealth by cheating people when collecting their taxes. In short (pun intended), he was a thief.

One day, Jesus came to Jericho. Zacchaeus wanted to simply get a look at this Jesus, whose reputation was growing. Unable to see over the crowd, little Zacchaeus climbed up into a tree. While up there, Jesus spotted him, called him by name, and *invited* himself over to stay at the tax collector's house. Many people grumbled and complained when they learned Jesus had "lowered" himself to stay with such a person (Zacchaeus was a thief, after all).

Jesus made such an impression on the little tax collector from Jericho that Zacchaeus pledged not only to pay back all those he had stolen from, but to pay four times what was taken! Huge change occurred that day in Zacchaeus. Why? He was set up to step up! His encounter with Jesus enabled him to receive a second chance at life—a fresh start. He was made new.

There are people all around you who are not very lovely or likeable, but remember: Jesus "came to seek and to save what was lost" (Luke 19:10). Be aware of those around you, the ONEs you don't think deserve another chance (you know who they are). Jesus wants you to partner with him in delivering an invitation for a fresh new start. What an opportunity!

By the way, don't expect everyone to understand or celebrate your association with people who have rough edges. Jesus was not applauded when he reached out to Zacchaeus, but aren't you glad that when you came up "short" Jesus was there for you?

Sorry for that last pun. Now, go and find your Zacchaeus.

Be Ready When God Moves

When I was serving at Valley Creek Church in Flower Mound, Texas, we had a New Member Experience for all the people interested in joining the church. It was a great time of food, information, discussion, and meeting new friends. There was also time for sharing the plan of salvation with those who might not know Christ. We talked about the importance of following through in believer's baptism, discipleship, and service to others.

After we dismissed one night, a man I had befriended approached me about being baptized. He was a local attorney named John who had recently given his heart to Christ but had not been baptized. God had used my testimony to help him see the importance of being scripturally baptized, and his concern was that he would be out of town the next Sunday.

John asked the question, "Is there any way I could be baptized tonight?"

Of course, immediately the details in my head clicked on: *Is there someone here to run the water? Do we have towels, clothes, and whatever else we need?* Then I quickly came to my senses. "Of course we can!"

It took awhile to get all the logistics worked out, so I made an announcement that John was going to be baptized. Three other people then came forward for baptism as well. That night was one of the highlights of my ministry at Valley Creek. Many people stayed around to celebrate, and we could all sense the smile of God. Because of John's willingness to be obedient to the Lord's command, we began offering baptism after every New Member Experience. We are so glad this precious man invited himself!

As you deepen and strengthen your relationship with your ONE, look for ways to show true hospitality. Look for ways to meet needs and create the space for a heart connection. Don't make your ONE invite him or herself— invite your ONE today.

ONE Focus Living—Real-Life Testimony
Cheryl

Shortly after I began working at a local dental office, the ONE Focus Initiative kicked off. I really didn't feel God had a strong presence in my workplace, although some people said that they went to church. Anyway, right away I knew who my ONE would be: a coworker named Trina.

I invited Trina to church occasionally, but I was not encouraged by her response at all. One time when I invited her to an Easter service, she replied, "Are you kidding me?" I understood her reluctance—that is a super crowded service.

I continued to pray after ONE Focus ended. God is so *good!* Trina softened over the years, and now I know we are friends, and more importantly, we are sisters in Christ.

Trina's mother-in-law was recently diagnosed with cancer, and after Trina's husband spent some extended time with his mom, he came back a believer! Trina was so confused, feeling that she would instantly have to change. I had a chance to sit with her and tell her that the Holy Spirit had been pursuing her for some time. It was *the* most precious moment as a believer to see her truly come to Christ.

After that, she would come to work and tell me with fascination of stories in the Bible—super cool! She has come to church a couple of times with me, and they do want to find a church home. Now she doesn't bite my head off if I say something about church. Instead, she wants to be a part of it!

On another note, my husband of three years, Brian, was Sherry's ONE (Sherry is another member of my church). Brian had been out of corporate fellowship for some time. Through Sherry, the Holy Spirit encouraged Brian to do just what he thought he would never do: go to the biggest church around!

Today Brian is such an awesome leader! He is serving as a deacon, a Kids Hope mentor, a volunteer at the thrift store once a month, and as a greeter, and he just has the biggest heart of a true servant.

God has blessed me so richly! I had given up on the thought of a husband to love me and my eighteen-year-old son, Cody, who is still at home. As God always does when you give it all to him, he gave me *so* much more than I would have ever dreamed or imagined! Oh yes, that also includes a precious daughter, Addison Grace, who is two years old. I even enjoy my work environment now because God is so present!

> He gave me so much more than I would have ever dreamed or imagined!

Thank you so much for letting me share my story. There is so much more detail of how God moved, but I tried to keep it short. Blessings and thank you!

ONE Focus Challenge

There are many ways to minister to your ONE with Christ's love. Think about the suggestions we have made, but also brainstorm your own ways to reach out in friendship and hospitality. Make a list of potential acts of love that match your personal talents and resources with your ONE's needs. Think beyond seeing eye to eye and look for ways to meet heart to heart.

Reflection

1. Is your home set up to receive guests?

   _____

   _____

   _____

2. If not, what makes you uncomfortable about having guests in your home?

   _____

   _____

   _____

   Take steps to make your home a place of hospitality, and invite your ONE over soon.

CHAPTER SEVEN

Storming the Gates

Simon Peter answered, "You are the Christ,
the Son of the living God." Jesus replied, "Blessed are you,
Simon son of Jonah, for this was not revealed to you by man,
but by my Father in heaven. And I tell you that you are
Peter, and on this rock I will build my church, and
the gates of Hades will not overcome it."
—Matthew 16:16–18

The Call

Bill sat and stared at the gun in his hand. He saw no reason to go on. Within the last three years, he had lost his job several times, he had struggled with illness, and—the hardest blow of all—his marriage had ended in divorce. Nothing was going right. Suicide seemed to be the only option.

It was then that Jimmy called Bill. You see, Bill was his ONE. Bill was also his brother. And Jimmy had no idea that this phone call would save his brother's life.

Jimmy had not only been praying for his brother's physical life but had committed to pray for his eternal life. For three years after Jimmy started ONE Focus, he demonstrated the love of Christ to his brother, prayed for him, and persistently invited him to attend church. Jimmy's small group had also reached out to him, trying to get him connected.

Through the ups and downs of Bill's life—including the night of the phone call that Bill later reported had deterred him from pulling the trigger—Jimmy was there for his younger brother. After three years, the wall came down, and both brothers sat in the pastor's office as Bill was led in a prayer of salvation. God had saved his life for all eternity.

That night as the pastor and two brothers stood before the church and shared the story, a group came forward to join them. These men and women were a part of Jimmy's small group who told how they had become involved in the life of this young man and his older brother's efforts for his salvation. As they were praying for Bill, God was also at work in their lives and hearts.

One man told of how he had been led to purchase a particular Bible for Bill, but when he went to the counter to pay, the cost was far beyond his price range. As he backed away, an older man who looked homeless came up to pay for his items and was several dollars short. The small group member felt led to give the money that was needed. After the man thanked him for his kindness, the clerk asked, "Which Bible was it you were wanting?" He explained he wanted the

Bible for someone who was not a Christian, but he could not afford the Bible he felt led to purchase. The clerk told him she had been given that exact Bible as an employee gift last week, would donate it, and would even engrave Bill's name on it as well.

Another person shared how God had impressed upon her to abstain from drinking Coke until Bill received salvation. A self-confessed soda pop addict, she at first argued with God about his "suggestion," but then faithfully went dry from that moment on. That night at church, she triumphantly popped open a soda. There was an air of celebration.

In the midst of this, and as more stories of the three-year period spent praying for Jimmy's ONE were shared, a lady walked forward and stood before the congregation. Surprised, the pastor stopped everything and asked if she needed help. The woman replied, "I want the joy I see in this new believer. What can I do to be saved?"

May the God who gives endurance and encouragement give you a spirit of unity among yourselves as you follow Christ Jesus, so that with ONE heart and mouth you may glorify the God and Father of our Lord Jesus Christ.
—Romans 15:5–6

Through the obedience of Jimmy and the others committed to showing God's love to Bill, multiple lives were changed forever. After the first woman came forward that night at church and asked what she could do to be saved, two more came—one for baptism and another for salvation. The story doesn't end there; Bill now has a testimony to share, and lives continue to be touched and changed.

It took over three years of praying and preparing while God orchestrated the steps of all those involved. Many lives were touched along the journey as efforts were made to bring this ONE man to Christ. This is only one example of God's faithfulness and how he hears the prayers of his people!

> *I urge, then, first of all, that requests, prayers,*
> *intercession and thanksgiving be made for everyone. . . .*
> *This is good, and pleases God our Savior, who*
> *wants all men to be saved and to come to a*
> *knowledge of the truth.*
> —1 Timothy 2: 1, 3–4

Prayer and ONE Focus

> *In every truly successful ministry,*
> *prayer is an evident and controlling force.*
> —E. M. Bounds

Prayer is the *most* important, mission-critical factor in the success of the ONE Focus Initiative. No great revival or movement has ever experienced true success without first establishing a strong ministry of prayer. If your church does not have a prayer ministry, maybe you are being led to begin one!

Many churches have prayer lists that include names of individuals with specific prayer needs. Most often, these lists do not include the names of those in need of salvation. There may be a prayer mentioned for the lost but no one specifically named. Learn to be specific and focused in your salvation prayers. If there is any fear of causing offense, use the initials of the lost individuals.

Prayer for the lost should be our top priority and the first item on all prayer lists. By simply having a salvation category on your prayer sheet, those in need of it are brought to the forefront of our minds, prayers, and actions. What we pray over will more likely be acted upon.

> Prayer is the most important, mission-critical factor in the success of the ONE Focus Initiative.

In Luke 11, Jesus instructs his disciples to pray, sending them out in pairs. They go out in praying partnership. In Matthew 18, we read that the prayers of two in agreement are granted by the Father. I encourage you once more to partner with someone else during ONE Focus, joining together in mutual support, accountability, and motivation.

When the disciples returned with good reports, Jesus gave thanks. Spiritual strength comes through prayer and will carry us through our efforts for Christ, and strength is also renewed through thanksgiving. Prayer is the number one priority at any successful church. The greater the prayer prominence, the greater the growth in discipleship and salvation. ONE Focus is relational, and *prayer is the greatest relational pathway to Christ.*

An Active Prayer Life

One good method for developing an active prayer life is to devote a particular period of the day to spending time with God in prayer and reflection. It's important to surround yourself with a spiritually healthy environment during work and free time (through books, music, television, friends, and so on), be actively involved in a body of believers, and live out your faith in your day-to-day life, but you must also cultivate your relationship with Christ. One of the keys to any solid relationship is commitment, and how do we show commitment? Through our time. Make sure you are not only asking God for direction, but taking the time to listen for how he replies. Prayer is the method that God established for communication with him, and it brings rest, guidance, joy, and peace.

> Prayer is the greatest relational pathway to Christ.

You can also get in the habit of praying throughout the day in response to whatever arises, whether it's the perfect parking spot on a rainy day or a terrible accident you pass on the interstate. Paul wrote in 1 Thessalonians 5:17 that we should "pray continually." Obviously, we cannot spend every moment of every day literally voicing prayers, but Paul was pointing toward a relationship with God in which we are in constant communion with him—continuously following his leadership, listening to his Spirit, giving our cares to him, and seeking his will for our lives. We do this through prayer.

The Power of Prayer

Over the years, I have made a practice of combining prayer and Scripture memorization. There are many stories I could share of God using prayer and his Word to move in powerful ways and reveal his guidance and presence. I want to share two experiences with you.

Lamar was one of the best soul-winners I have ever known. He was a bold and gifted man of God who made witnessing seem easy. Lamar and I were friends, until one day when I had to confront him over an issue. It was a sad and difficult situation, and Lamar quit attending the church where I served.

One morning, months later, I was praying and memorizing Matthew 4:19, "'Come, follow me,' Jesus said, 'and I will make you fishers of men.'" As I repeated that verse, my old friend Lamar's face came to my mind. Lamar was a "fisher of men." I had not seen or heard from him in months, but later that night at our Wednesday night church activities, guess who I saw? I walked up to Lamar, told him how glad I was to see him, and explained how the Lord had brought him to mind that morning as I was memorizing Matthew 4:19.

When I said this, Lamar got really excited and told me that Matthew 4:19 was his life verse, which God had given him years ago. He had even written that verse on the concrete floor of the new worship center before the carpet was laid. What a celebration of God's Word and power we had that night!

Here's another story of God's faithfulness through prayer and Scripture: One morning during my time with the Lord, I was memorizing Philippians 4:6–7, "Do not be anxious about anything, but in everything, by prayer and petition, with thanksgiving, present your requests to God. And the peace of God, which transcends all understanding, will guard your hearts and your minds in Christ Jesus." It happened to be a Sunday morning, and I was practicing my memorization in the car with Cindy on the way to church.

We had three worship services each morning, and after the second one had started, I was in the foyer of the church visiting with a few volunteers. A friend of mine named Monroe walked toward me in a panic and insisted on talking to me immediately. He asked to speak to me privately, so I was a little nervous about what he was going to say.

I found a private place and Monroe told me had been diagnosed with colon cancer. He had already begun treatment; he was not feeling well and was very discouraged. In fact, he was not planning on attending church that day; he had intended to stay home and watch our live broadcast on television. He said that as he was watching the program, God spoke to his heart, telling him to go to church because God had given *me* a word to share with him!

Can you imagine the pressure I felt? For a moment I had no idea what to say, and then I knew—Philippians 4:6–7. Monroe began to weep as I quoted the verse. I prayed over him and asked God to give him the peace of that verse!

Praying for Your ONE

Prayer is not only the greatest tool we have for a deeper relationship with Christ, it is also our most powerful instrument for reaching the lost. As you develop your relationship with your ONE, do not neglect an active prayer life—it is the most crucial part of any evangelism. You should pray for your ONE daily, and as you get to know your ONE better, you can pray for your ONE's specific needs. Here are some other ideas for how to pray for your ONE:

- Pray that your paths will cross often and your words and actions will be guided by God.
- Ask God to help you build trust with your ONE.
- Pray for common interests or an opening in conversation about spiritual things.
  - "This is what we speak, not in words taught us by human wisdom but in words taught by the Spirit, expressing spiritual truths in spiritual words" (1 Cor. 2:13).
- Ask God to help you encourage and affirm your ONE.
- Ask God to help you model victorious living to your ONE.
- Pray for your ONE's eyes to be opened to God's love, creation, and power.
- Pray for your ONE's family.
- Pray for your ONE's salvation, asking the Holy Spirit to work in his or her life.
- Pray you will become aware of situations in which you can minister to your ONE's family.
- Pray for opportunities to invite your ONE to church.
- Pray for an open door to share your testimony.
- Pray for the right time to present God's plan of salvation.
- Pray for your ONE's eyes and ears to be open to the Gospel of Jesus Christ.

Jesus and Prayer

Before his arrest, Jesus prayed for himself, his disciples, and then for all the believers:

> *My prayer is not for them alone. I pray also for those who will believe in me through their message that all of them may be ONE, Father, just as you are in me and I am in you. May they also be in us so that the world may believe that you have sent me. I have given them the glory that you gave me, that they may be ONE as we are ONE: I in them and you in me. May they be brought to complete unity to let the world know that you sent me and have loved them even as you have loved me* (John 17:20–23, emphasis added).

Complete unity—what an incredible thought! "That they be ONE as we are ONE." A prayer request of Jesus when he was days away from being crucified was that we would be so close to the Father and other believers that the whole world would know God sent Jesus. Complete unity—how about it?

In His Hands

Cindy

Having served as a children's minister for many years, my greatest joy has always been talking with boys and girls about becoming a Christian. There are so many ways to share the plan of salvation and each child has a different learning style. Some are quiet and thoughtful, others cannot stop talking. You have probably read some of the funny things children have said about God—I can assure you I have had to laugh out loud several times. Other times, I have shed happy tears.

There was one little girl I will never forget. She gave an insight from her childlike faith. She had become a Christian, but her parents were concerned because she had asked Jesus to come into her heart twice. We went back over the plan of salvation and her commitment prayer. I showed her the verse in John 10:28: "I give them eternal life, and they shall never perish; no one can snatch them out of my hand."

As I held out my hand and asked if she could imagine how safe it would be in Jesus' hand, she said, "Yes, Mrs. Cindy, that is why I asked him twice—because I wanted to be in *both* his hands!"

I would like to be in both of Jesus' hands, too, and I would like to bring others with me. Will you pray that your ONE feels our Lord's hands in his or her life, and that the Lord uses you to reach your ONE?

ONE Focus Living—Real-Life Testimony
Pastor Cyle Clayton

I cannot overemphasize the importance of prayer before, during, and after ONE Focus. I am convinced that the prayer focus prior to the launch of ONE Focus at our church was the reason it was so successful—when we were praying, God was moving. I believe you should do it by the book as much as possible. If you have to let something slide, do not let it be prayer. When we prayed, we saw people saved. When we didn't, we didn't.

It's not about the act of praying. It's about our dependence upon God and our faith in him. The person who believes that God can and will do great things prays greatly.

ONE Focus Challenge

The Prayer Dare
Dr. Michael Walker

I f you want to see Christ move in your life, take this Prayer Dare. Such a dare involves a ten-ten-ten exercise for ten days:

- Read your Bible for ten minutes.
- Pray for ten minutes.
- Be silent and still for ten minutes.

Will you do this for ten consecutive days? At the end of the ten days, conclude with prayer and reflection on what God has taught you.

Reflection

1. Be sure your conversation with God is not one-sided. When you pray, are you listening for God's response?

    _____

    _____

    _____

2. Has there been a major event in your life through which God has answered prayer? What did you learn from the experience?

    _____

    _____

    _____

CHAPTER EIGHT

Salt and Light

ONE Focus Living—Real-Life Testimony

Jennifer

My ONE came into my life a little more than seven years ago. When I heard about ONE Focus at our church, I knew right away that Shawn was my ONE. I knew that I would pray for him without ceasing. Though my pastor said that our ONE should probably not be someone of the opposite sex, Shawn had come into my life through my niece, who had a relationship with him. I knew that I could pray for both of them to come to know Christ; however, the Holy Spirit urged me that Shawn was my ONE.

This young man had a beautiful heart, but he placed a powerful shield around it and would only drop it occasionally. He had grown up in a broken home, fought for his place in life, and come to believe that he was a misfit. As I watched him from a distance, my heart broke for him. The wounds from his past would often explode in bursts of anger. He sought escape in drug and alcohol abuse. As I watched him travel down this dark road, I continually asked God to save him.

Unfortunately, Shawn and my niece had a baby out of wedlock. Mistakenly, I thought that the birth of this beautiful little girl might serve as the catalyst to turn around Shawn's life. The responsibility of his child and his relationship with my niece, though, only created more stress. His life spiraled deeper into darkness and even worse habits formed, which eventually resulted in his arrest and conviction. Shawn spent eighteen months in prison.

During this time, he went to three different prisons in Louisiana. He said that he did not want to make a "jailhouse confession" and blow it when he was released; however, he did start seeking the Lord while in prison. He faced many challenging and humiliating circumstances, but in all of them, he prayed and gave God thanks.

Toward the end of his sentence, Shawn got the chance to participate in a work-release program through which God put him in the hands of a family in the area who owned a farm and a roofing company. The Lord used this godly family to draw Shawn into the Kingdom. One evening each week, they would keep him in their home through dinner. Afterward, he would sit with this family to pray and to talk about life. This family demonstrated God's grace and mercy, and they showed him what a loving family looks like.

Once he had served his time, he had no home to which he could return, no job, and no transportation. That all changed. As we prayed about his circumstances, God blessed him yet again. My husband and I invited him into our home, his grandfather gave him an old but reliable pickup truck, and within a couple of weeks, he had a good job. I know that God provided Shawn with all of this.

About this time, I made a public commitment to pray earnestly for, serve, and look for witnessing opportunities for my ONE, Shawn. As you might expect, Satan tried to keep Shawn away from God. Within a few months, Shawn's old habits surfaced. I knew that I had to keep praying for him and loving him in Christ.

The day Shawn finally gave control of his life to Christ gave me the most wonderful joy. I am so thankful that God used me in this young man's life and allowed me to point out God's hand in all things. He used me, my family, and my church to make an eternal difference.

By the way, my niece came to know Christ several months prior to Shawn's conversion. She has followed the Lord in baptism. What an awesome God! To him, I give all the glory!

Salt and Light

You are the salt of the earth. But if the salt loses its saltiness, how can it be made salty again? It is no longer good for anything, except to be thrown out and trampled by men. You are the light of the world. A city on a hill cannot be hidden.
—Matthew 5:13–14

It is so exciting to see new Christians. They are on fire for God and ready to tell everyone the Good News. Think back on the time you accepted Christ as your personal Lord and Savior. You felt new, fresh, and ready to take on the world. But what happens after a few weeks or a few months? Do we lose our saltiness? Does our light grow dim?

There is an object lesson I have used with children and youth to demonstrate this point. Giving each person a stick of gum, I would ask, "How does the gum taste?" The kids would respond, "Full of flavor," "Sweet," and so on. At the end of the hour, I would ask, "How does the gum taste now?" The response was not the same; it had lost its flavor. It is easy to become that way as Christians. We may be full of flavor and excitement for Christ, but then after time, we begin to go through the motions—not being effective or tasting the goodness of the Lord.

God tells us to be salt and light to the earth. Salt preserves and enhances what it is applied to; therefore, we must preserve and enhance what is good in our communities. As salt alters the flavor of food, we are called to season and affect where God calls us. We have to accept the challenge to share with others so that we will not lose our saltiness. Likewise, light chases away the darkness and brings insight and direction. We must scatter the darkness with our love, illuminate the path for others, and be a reflection of Christ. Being salt and light means being a witness and testimony to impact our society with goodness and kindness.

Real Evangelism Is Showing Love

It couldn't be any clearer. In the Bible, we are told this: God is love. If we are to be his representatives on Earth, we must live out his love on a daily basis. And ultimately, it is this love that will draw in the lost, and it is this love that will touch the heart of your ONE. I think the best thing to do at this point is to tell you a few stories—stories about love. These are stories of being salt and light to the world.

Dear friends, let us love one another, for love comes from God. Everyone who loves has been born of God and knows God. Whoever does not love does not know God, because God is love. This is how God showed his love among us: He sent his one and only Son into the world that we might live through him. This is love: not that we loved God, but that he loved us and sent his Son as an atoning sacrifice for our sins.
—1 John 4:7–10

The Peppermint Pastor

Cindy and I had been at First Baptist Church for a long time; Cindy had been there since she was in the sixth grade. She began volunteering when she was in junior high and was now the Mother's Day Out coordinator. Our children, who were four and seven, had been in the church nursery since they were three weeks old, and they participated in everything available. Our friends and many family members attended there, and we loved our pastor, Dr. Clifton Tennison. Dr. T, as we lovingly called him, had been at FBC for twenty-nine years.

I wish you could hear his voice—it was one of the gentlest, deepest, warmest voices you have ever heard. Cindy and I have both had dreams about him. When we were beginning ONE Focus, Dr. T had already gone home to heaven, and I had a very vivid dream where he came to me and said, "This is not going to be easy. You are going to have lots and lots of meetings. There will be many things to do. Don't get discouraged."

Cindy remembers this about him:

Dr. Clifton Tennison was known and loved for many reasons. I will always remember one special thing about him. My family had moved from Kentucky and we were looking for a church home. We had visited other churches but my brother and I wanted to go back to the place with the "Peppermint Pastor." Senior Pastor Dr. Tennison would stand at the door and give out peppermints after the worship service. He connected with the people during that time with his warm smile and handshake. It was his way of building a relationship with the many families at church. It worked for us; we joined the church and became lifelong friends with the Tennison family. After Dr. T went to be with Jesus, one of the precious men in the church took over the peppermint patrol!

Dr. T showed love in so many ways, and he continues to encourage us even though he passed away several years ago. A few months back, Cindy and I both woke up one morning after an unusually disappointing week. I looked at

Cindy and said, "I dreamed about Dr. T," and she said, "I did, too." We went on to explain the dreams to each other and they were of him standing there in the background, smiling a reassuring smile, as if to say, "It is OK, keep going, keep striving, it will come together."

It did come together—we kept striving, and God has been continually faithful—and through his demonstrations of love, our beloved "Peppermint Pastor" continues to inspire us to love others.

The Chapel Steps

Love your neighbor as yourself.
—Mark 12:31

First Baptist Church was established in a downtown area of West Monroe. There were many families around the church in low socioeconomic situations, and we often had trouble with children entering the building unsupervised. We would invite them to our services, but it seemed they only wanted to be there when they were not allowed—typical for any children roaming a neighborhood and looking for something to do!

The biggest temptation was a large gymnasium with a full basketball court, which they passed by each day and could look inside but were not allowed to enjoy. Looking back now, we realize the evangelistic opportunity and wonder why it took so many years to see the mission field in which God had placed us.

After several incidents and many complaints from

church members, we knew something had to be done. One day after school, I saw a group of young boys riding their bikes up and down the outside steps of the chapel. My first reaction was the imperfect, human one—I was worried that they would damage the chapel columns or be injured themselves. Immediately after, though, I felt convicted to talk to them about the Lord. Miraculously, I corralled them; most of the time they just ran from me—and they ran fast! That day, they listened as I shared the Good News and all four boys were saved.

A couple of months later, I baptized two of the boys, the first African-Americans ever baptized at First West. This was the catalyst to launch a neighborhood ministry called F.A.N. (Friends and Neighbors) Club. The children came on Saturday mornings to play in the gym, participate in crafts, engage in a Bible study, and receive a sack lunch. Most weeks we had over 150 children and 20–30 volunteers. Our lifelong friends, Ken and Terra Taylor, faithfully led this ministry for over twenty years.

F.A.N. Club has been an integral part of the community transformation that has taken place. Through this ministry, a thrift store was established to help meet the physical needs of local families. Kids Hope, a tutoring program designed to assist boys and girls with their academic needs, was also formed. Thousands of boys and girls have been impacted, as well as their families, because a church took seriously the command "Love your neighbor."

Miss Nell

Love the Lord your God with all
your heart and with all your soul and with all
your mind and with all your strength.
—Mark 12:30

Miss Nell Odom was one of those ladies who made an impression on every person she met. She had a smile that covered her face and reached right up to her eyes. You could tell she loved Jesus just by looking at her, but she was also quick to share her testimony of his love and grace.

No one was a stranger to Miss Nell, and we all loved listening to her stories of years gone by. She was a widow who especially enjoyed talking about her beloved husband. They had been married for forty-two years before he died of pancreatic cancer at the age of sixty-four. One of their daughters, Jackie, told me that her mom loved to dance around the living room with her dad, and that her eyes always sparkled when she looked at him.

Love was part of the family inheritance. Another daughter, Deb, remembers: "My grandmother is where Mama learned to give, pray, and serve. Even in her early nineties, my grandmother took food to people and visited the elderly (we never could figure out if she knew that *she* was elderly!). She and my grandfather served in their church faithfully. They were a living example for my mom, as Mama was for us."

Miss Nell picked up quickly on the interests and needs of others. For example, I do not eat much sugar, so each time she made an angel food cake, she would make a small sugar-free one for me. When she found out our son and daughter liked her fudge pies, she began making each of them a birthday pie. She first started making a pie for my daughter, Jenny, but when Jake found out, he quickly let her know when his birthday was. Our children loved Miss Nell just like everyone else did.

Miss Nell volunteered for every activity involving people in need. She cooked, cleaned, sewed and sorted clothes, taught classes, and prepared arts and crafts. She rocked babies, disciplined young boys, and took young girls grocery shopping. In her earlier years, she taught VBS and was president of the PTA at her daughters' school.

Miss Nell was always there to serve others. Jesus would not have to ask her more than once if she loved him! Her actions were proof. She was part of a prayer team called Aaron's Army that met at 7:30 each Sunday morning to pray for the staff before services and then prayer walk the building. Miss Nell loved to pray over the children's area, and she was always there for prayer, even when she did not feel well.

Miss Nell had suffered with esophageal cancer once before and beat it, but a few years ago, it returned and spread to her lungs. Many of us told her that she was "the most beautiful bald woman" we had ever seen. Sometimes she wore big floppy hats or caps. Even during this time, Miss Nell remained faithful to church and most of her activities.

During ONE Focus, Miss Nell was a committed participant. It came naturally to her, because she had practiced it all her life. She loved the Lord with all her heart, soul, mind, and strength, and now she is living with him eternally.

Miss Nell had a daily, active relationship with God. We were created to have that kind of relationship with God, the all-powerful Creator who was and is and is to come. His presence

> God wants his children to enter into a love relationship with him.

is everywhere. He created all things, knows all things, and has perfect wisdom. The Bible presents him as one God in three persons: Father, Son, and Holy Spirit.

God wants his children to enter into a love relationship with him. While I have already written about this, it bears repeating: If you love someone, you spend time with that person—you have a growing, personal relationship. Spending time in prayer, Bible study, and quiet time with God demonstrates your love. If you do not have a regularly scheduled quiet time, begin *today.* God's Word is alive and active, demonstrating the power to move someone from the depths of despair to the heights of peace and joy.

Even though there are thousands of devotional books available, the most important thing one can do is pray, read Scripture, and then *listen.* Using a journal to record thoughts is also a helpful way to keep the communication going. You can read a proverb or a psalm each day for wisdom and encouragement. One good way to study is to research a topic and read verses pertaining to that subject. You will soon look forward to the time and not want to miss it—God has much he wants to share with you personally.

A Katrina Memory
Vincent L. Nzinga

God put it on my heart to prepare an emergency plan as the church administrator of Franklin Avenue Baptist Church of New Orleans. My first thought was this: If a horrific event occurred in New Orleans, could the people survive? Through my meetings with the Red Cross Agency, they informed us that should a storm come into New Orleans from a certain direction, thousands of people could lose their lives to flood water. The Agency concluded that New Orleans lacked transportation to move large numbers, and no buildings would be safe as shelters because they would become islands surrounded by water from the Gulf of Mexico.

It became clear to me that we needed a plan should such a catastrophe of that magnitude strike New Orleans. A plan was prepared and our senior pastor, Dr. Fred Luter Jr., gave the names of three churches that we should contact as potential shelters. First Baptist Church of West Monroe was one of those churches. We contacted Sue Griffin at that church, and she immediately said yes. She also said, "Now all I have to do is get the pastor to say the same."

The Saturday before Katrina decided to take aim at New Orleans, I gave Sue a call and informed her that we were headed her way.

Fear of the Unknown
On the road to West Monroe, the racial factor became prominent in our minds. Franklin Avenue is basically black and First West is basically white. We had heard all the sto-

ries of how whites of northern Louisiana had disdain for blacks—particularly blacks from southern Louisiana.

My family was the first to arrive and we made arrangements to meet Sue Griffin, who turned out to be a pint-sized white woman, probably born in the '40s like me, who must have understood the racial segregation that divided this state for many years. We were apprehensive and we figured that she was, too, meeting a black family at close to midnight on a deserted back street under the steeple of First West. But as soon as we made eye contact with this woman, our fear of the unknown vanished immediately. With her northern "Louziana drawl," she said, "You must be Vince," and with a "Nawlins" accent I gave the reply, "You must be Sue." From that point on, Sue and my family became the best of friends.

The People Came

The next morning, the people begin to arrive. Amazingly, First West sprang into action. We saw an abundance of passionate people making their way to the church with cots,

> We were in desperate need of everything, and God's family responded. The blessings poured out.

inflatable mattresses, soft drinks, blankets, cases of water, food of all types, and—matter of fact—a statement was made that we didn't know white folks could cook as well as we can. A lot of fears were dispelled during the awful times of Katrina. The people of Franklin Avenue and First West truly became sisters and brothers.

When we realized that Katrina was not going to be a three-day event, both First West and Franklin Avenue began to organize specific committees: education, medical, recreation, sanitation, and housing. We were in desperate need of everything, and God's family responded. The blessings poured out: our kids missed only one day of school, and all school districts were opened to us; a local pharmacist provided us with medication; the youth of the church instructed our kids in recreation; we policed our shelter and kept it sanitized; and all our people were placed into first-class housing within three weeks of the devastation of New Orleans.

Blessings

A great number of the people from First West approached me and politely told me that they were blessed by meeting the people of Franklin Avenue, because they had such limited opportunities to meet so many black people at one time, and as a result of these encounters, many of their fears had dissolved. We went on to develop individual friendships; in fact, my family and a family we met during that time still communicate with each other today. A Sunday doesn't pass in church that someone doesn't come up to me and ask or tell me something about someone at First West.

We realized that we are all God's children.

Dear friends, since God so loved us,
we also ought to love one another. No one has
ever seen God; but if we love one another, God lives
in us and his love is made complete in us.
—1 John 4:11–12

ONE Focus Challenge

Remember that it is all about love. Pray that your ONE comes to experience the greatest love of all, and that if the time comes that your ONE is ready to hear the Gospel, you will be prepared to share it and to give the testimony for what God has done in your life.

While you deepen your relationship with your ONE, will you also look for opportunities to be salt and light to others around you? I challenge you to commit to seek out opportunities daily to show God's love, in small or large ways, to all the people whose paths will cross yours, even for only a moment. Do not let a single chance to impact someone's life through love go by.

Do all the good you can, by all the means you can,
in all the ways you can, in all the places you can,
at all the times you can, to all the people
you can, as long as ever you can.
—Commonly attributed to John Wesley

Reflection

Gary Chapman, in his best-selling book *The Five Love Languages,* describes the common "love languages"—the primary ways that individuals express and interpret love. Although Chapman's focus is on romantic love, we all respond to acts of love—thoughtfulness, kindness, or compassion—within a friendship in a variety of ways.

1. What type of words or actions within a friendship would mean the most to you?

    _____

    _____

    _____

2. What type of words or actions do you think would mean the most to your ONE?

    _____

    _____

    _____

CHAPTER NINE

By the Blood and the Word

ONE Focus Living—Real-Life Testimony
Dr. Michael Walker

One night, years ago, I had a dream. In my dream, I had died and was arriving into heaven. As I walked on clouds approaching heaven's entrance, Jesus came out to meet me. As he approached, I could see his eyes looking behind me to see who I had brought with me—whom I had shared him with, how I had taken part in telling his story. At that time in my life, I had not shared salvation with anyone. Oh, I had taken my family to church, taught a small group, and been active in church business, but I had failed to tell others of him.

As I looked upon Jesus and he searched, seeing no one behind me, I could see the brokenness of his heart. Though his expression never changed, it was as though I looked into his very soul. I saw his hurt over my failure. I saw how much my never sharing had disappointed him. I saw my failures somehow projected onto him.

When I woke up, I vowed not to have what I experienced in that dream become real. I promised myself that many would hear and come to know him. I would not be silent, hushed, or still until all the world had heard.

> I pray that if you are living only as a believer, you will promise to grow into a disciple.

I pray that if you are living only as a believer, you will promise to grow into a disciple. I pray that you will not be silent or indifferent over unsaved people and that a great crowd will follow you into heaven one day as a result of sharing his love. All people need to meet Christ, and it is your responsibility to see that they do. Someone is waiting for you to share the love of Christ. Will you?

True Fellowship

We proclaim to you what we have seen
and heard, so that you also may have fellowship
with us. And our fellowship is with the Father
and with his Son, Jesus Christ. We write
this to make our joy complete.
—1 John 1:3–4

After you have built a relationship with your ONE and are ready to talk about spiritual things, this verse is a perfect explanation of why we want him or her to know about Jesus. We want to share the wonderful fellowship we have in Christ so our joy together will be complete, but do not rush it. A person will listen to a friend, whereas they will ignore a stranger. Become a friend before you share.

We should be very eager to tell our friends and family about the wonderful saving knowledge of Jesus Christ. This is the most rewarding experience we can have! Christians in fellowship with Christ bring joy to us and to God.

Talking with others who don't know Jesus is always risky, but it is worth the risk to bring the complete joy of fellowship. As you spend time together, a relationship will develop and grow that will usher in a perfect time of sharing. Sharing Jesus with a stranger is difficult, but sharing Jesus with a friend comes more easily. Will you be bold for Christ today?

> **Will you be bold for Christ today?**

Your Personal Testimony

Your personal testimony is a very powerful tool. Revelation 12:11 says, "They overcame him [Satan] by the blood of the Lamb and the word of their testimony."

Look at the next two Scriptures:

> *You will be his witness to all men of*
> *what you have seen and heard."*
> —Acts 22:15

*Anyone who believes in the Son of God has this
testimony in his heart. Anyone who does not believe has
made him out to be a liar, because he has not believed the
testimony God has given about his Son.*
—1 John 5:10

Cindy gives this example of using her personal testimony:
Many times I have used my testimony when people of other
faiths have tried to sway my thoughts or beliefs. When they
try to confuse me with their smooth words or conflicting
verses, to which I do not have an immediate answer, I
always go back to my personal experience. I say, "I may not
be able to quote Scripture and tell you the exact places in the
Bible to find the answers I know are there, but let me tell you
what Christ has done in my life personally." I have never had
anyone argue with that.

Like the covering blood of Christ, the word of your
personal experience is something no one can take away
from you. It is your best evangelism tool, and it is unique
to you.

Who Are You?
Cindy

When you are asked that question, what is your response? I usually say, "I am Scotty's wife," or "Jenny
and Jake's mom," or "Abby Grace, Ashlyn, Jillian Kate, and
Jessa-Claire's Gigi." I might answer that I am "Jay and Rose-
mary's daughter," or "Brad's sister." My family is very impor-

tant to me. However, my personal identity should be based on who I am in Christ.

Use the following Bible verses to provide a basis for living a successful, triumphant life in him, and share that life with others!

Who I Am In Christ

I am a child of God
—John 1:12

I am a friend of Christ
—John 15:15

I am part of the body of Christ
—1 Corinthians 12:27

I have access to God
—Ephesians 2:18

I have been forgiven
—Colossians 1:14

I cannot be separated from the love of God
—Romans 8:35–39

I am a personal witness of Christ
—Acts 1:8

I am God's workmanship
—Ephesians 2:10

I am the salt and light of the earth
—Matthew 5:13–14

Your Testimony Has Power

God tells us our testimony is powerful, so we should be ready to use it. Webster's definition of testimony is "any form of evidence or declaration in support of truth." In Acts 26, Paul gives testimony to King Agrippa of a changed life because of Jesus Christ. Imprisoned and on trial before the King, Paul describes how Christ had turned his life around, and he concludes his testimony by saying, "I pray God that not only you but all who are listening to me today may become what I am, except for these chains" (Acts 26:29). His witness was a powerful tool then and continues to inspire us today.

What about your testimony? If you have received Christ as your personal Lord and Savior, then you have a story to tell. In a court of law, a witness is called to give testimony of what he or she knows as truth. It is easy to be a witness for Christ—just tell what Jesus has done for you personally.

Here are some ideas to get you started. When you become a Christian:

- You have not seen the risen Lord, but you know he is alive because he changes you on the inside.
- Jesus has forgiven your sins and lives in your heart.
- God is preparing a place in heaven for you and all who will receive him.
- God is working in your life each day (give examples when witnessing to someone).
- You feel God's presence, peace, and joy even in the midst of crisis.
- God gives his Holy Spirit to guide you.
- God answers your prayers and speaks to you through his Word.

Be Prepared to Share

God tells us in 1 Peter 3:15 to "always be prepared to give an answer to everyone who asks you to give the reason for the hope that you have. But do this with gentleness and respect."

It is a good idea to write out your testimony and practice it so you will be ready to share when God gives you an opportunity. Before you begin, pray and ask God to guide you as you prepare the words.

Essential Helps

- Be honest; do not exaggerate or try to make your story more dramatic. The Holy Spirit will use your words to touch hearts.
- Be current. Tell what God is doing in your life today.
- Do not use "churchy" words or clichés a non-follower of Christ may not understand.
- Emphasize the positive and focus on God's faithfulness.
- Identify with your ONE and select statements about yourself that will help this person relate to your life.
- Give your testimony in about three minutes.

Other Guidelines

- Pray and ask God to lead you.
- Think about your life before you became a Christian. What was going on in your life? What problems were you facing?
- Start with a simple outline:
  - Before I received Christ . . .
  - How I received Christ . . .
  - Since I received Christ . . .

An Example

- Before I asked Jesus to be my Savior I . . .
  - ° What were you searching for? What was the key problem, emotion, or attitude you were dealing with? Share something about your past that shows you were a sinner.
- Then one day I . . .
  - ° Where were you? What was happening at the time? Who or what influenced your decision to consider Christ as the solution to your searching?
- Since Jesus has saved me . . .
  - ° How has your life changed because of Christ's forgiveness? What is Jesus doing in your life today?

After you have given your testimony, ask if you can share the plan of salvation. That is the next step and your ONE may be ready. Do not be discouraged if your ONE does not respond—the Holy Spirit is working and you have fulfilled your responsibility. Keep praying and God will continue to give you opportunities to share.

Hold on to this promise: "On the day he comes to be glorified in his holy people and to be marveled at among all those who have believed. This includes you, because you believed our testimony to you" (2 Thes. 1:10).

> Keep praying and God will continue to give you opportunities to share.

Killing Our Witness

Pastor Cyle Clayton

> *Meanwhile a large crowd of Jews found out that*
> *Jesus was there and came, not only because of Jesus, but*
> *also to see Lazarus, the one he had raised from the dead.*
> *So the chief priests decided to kill Lazarus as well, for on*
> *account of him many of the Jews were going over to*
> *Jesus and putting their faith in him.*
> —John 12:9–10

We're not supposed to be self-esteem junkies. We don't need to get up every morning, look in the mirror, and say, "I'm good enough, I'm smart enough, and doggone it, people like me." However, you should know something: you are precious to God and so is your witness for him. God loved you while you were yet a sinner, while your witness was actually against him. He loves you now as a son, a daughter. He doesn't just love you because you can do something for him. Anything we could do for him, he could do better. Yet he values your witness.

Your ability to give glory to God, as a child of God through faith in Jesus Christ, is a limited commodity and is precious to God. Satan knows this, and he does not want sinners saved by grace to bear witness to their Savior. Satan cannot change your status as a child of God—that is sealed in Christ—but he can affect your witness. He makes every effort to do so, just like he used the chief priests in an attempt to kill not only Jesus but also Lazarus.

There are two ways to lose your witness. You, all by yourself, can just blow it. While born again, you still live in a fallen body. Your own desires, your own belief that you can live one moment apart from the sustaining power of Christ, can lead you to blow it—quickly. You can also be attacked. We don't need help blowing it, but there is help. Powers of darkness and spiritual forces of evil are aligned against us. They want us to blow our witness.

So, *don't* blow it. How? Whether it is your sinful nature, a seductive temptation, or an onslaught by the prince of darkness, the answer is the same: stay close to Christ. Abide in him, early, regularly, and all day. One step without him is one step on the wrong road. Your victory is not in you, or in your strength, so stay close to Christ, his Word, and his example.

No, get closer . . . nope, not close enough. Get closer still.

ONE Focus Challenge

Write out your testimony this week, and then be prepared to share it when God gives you the opportunity. Practice with your accountability partner, a friend, or someone else with whom you feel very comfortable. The only bad testimony is the one never given. God has a way of blessing our efforts on his behalf to give glorious results, so trust him to be with you and speak through your voice. The fact that you care enough to share is a powerful tool in itself; such love will reap miracles. ONE Focus allows a full year to find your ONE, develop a true relationship, and eventually share your testimony. Do not procrastinate, but also do not feel pressured or rushed. Let God guide your timing. This book presents a year of equipping in just a few weeks, so use it as needed along the way. You will need to refer to this book as your harvest becomes ripe for gathering.

Reflection

1. What are your greatest fears about sharing your testimony with others? Pray that God would give you peace and confidence regarding these fears.

   _____

   _____

   _____

2. Has God ever impressed on you the need to give your testimony, and did you follow through? If yes, how did it go? If no, what kept you from sharing?

   _____

   _____

   _____

CHAPTER TEN

The Greatest Gift

ONE Focus Living—Real-Life Testimony
Judy Groll

When investing in someone's life, sometimes you don't know the outcome or the effect your encounter had on that person's life until months or years later—or maybe never at all! The purpose behind ONE Focus, for me, was to see people grow closer to God and to learn to approach each day thinking of someone other than myself. I not only witnessed ONE Focus change the lives of individuals outside the walls of the church, I witnessed ONE Focus change my life as well.

Years after the initial vision of ONE Focus was developed and established in our ministry, the change in my approach to ministering to others remains a life-changing mandate within my heart that still resonates today. Learning to wake up each morning and not look at what I can do for myself, but what I can do to make a difference in someone else's life—it has been rewarding, to say the least.

Walking up to someone's door and knocking time and time again to share the Gospel was difficult for me. On most nights, I didn't want someone coming to my door when I was spending time with my family or eating dinner, so in my opinion, why would I interrupt other people's lives, not respecting their family time, and expect them to accept what I had to offer? Even though I was sharing the greatest gift of all, my confidence level was low because I was out of my comfort zone.

> With ONE Focus, I discovered I was able to show Christ more effectively.

With ONE Focus, I discovered I was able to show Christ more effectively through my actions of love and consideration for each person with whom I came into contact on a daily basis. Whether for one day or five to ten years, being consistent in caring for someone has left more of an impact, and opened more doors to sharing the love of Christ, than any impact I may have made doing something as simple (but uncomfortable to me) as knocking on a door. For some individuals the door-to-door approach may be a realistic and effective way to minister, but for me, that method was not working.

Whether visiting with a waitress at a restaurant week after week for years, baking cookies and meals for a neighbor who lives alone, opening our home to a family who needed somewhere to stay, or praying with someone in the parking lot at a local department store, I found out investment opportunities are everywhere—and it is really not difficult to find them! Finding one person at a time to invest in has made discipleship simple for me. I have seen hearts change because of the time and effort put into people's lives, whether it was me or someone I know who went through the ONE Focus training. Once the vision "clicked," lives started changing for good. As I wake up each morning praying for the people I meet and those God may place in my life, a peace comes to me to just follow Christ and know that he will lead the way. This is a far cry from where my thoughts were before ONE Focus.

Truly, giving to others is more of a blessing than receiving, and along the way, Christ is there to guide and direct every step of your day. Looking back, I can see where God handpicked everyone with whom a relationship was built. Thinking it was me who found them was ridiculous; I just needed to recognize their existence and need. *All along the way he put each ONE in my path* . . . and for that I am *eternally* grateful.

If you have a solid foundation in God's Word and an ongoing, dynamic relationship with him, you'll feel empowered to take the next step in your relationship with your ONE. You can share your testimony, and when the time is right, tell your ONE how to receive the gift Christ offers—the greatest gift of all.

Before we talk about sharing the Gospel and extending an invitation to accept Christ as Lord, let's take a moment to reconsider what is at stake.

Heaven and Hell

Dr. Michael Walker

What will heaven be like? Here are a few things the Bible tells us about what heaven will be like:
- We will be like Jesus!
  - "Dear friends, now we are children of God, and what we will be has not yet been made known. But we know that when he appears, we shall be like him, for we shall see him as he is" (1 John 3:2).
- We will no longer sin!
  - "Being confident in this, that he who began a good work in you will carry it on to completion until the day of Christ Jesus" (Phil. 1:6).
- We will be with Christ!
  - "They will see his face, and his name will be on their foreheads" (Rev. 22:4).

Imagine a ONE reunion when we see Christ face-to-face. There is no sun or moon because the radiance of his glory is all the light needed. We stand on streets of gold and precious gems with the River of Life providing a backdrop for the angels singing. We can only imagine how beautiful it will be.

The Opportunity to Choose

Besides receiving the eternal presence of God as believers, we are spared eternal damnation and separation from him. I think we neglect to focus on the fact that there are only two choices—heaven or hell. Failing to choose heaven is the choice of hell. Don't all people deserve the opportunity to choose for themselves? When we do not fulfill our responsibility to share the Gospel with others, is that in some way choosing for

> Failing to choose heaven is the choice of hell.

them? We, each one of us, will be held accountable for what we did with our free gift of salvation.

Salvation

Do you think of your salvation and eternal life as a gift? Do you treat your salvation that way?

We do not have to make an appointment with the pastor or repeat a special prayer after one of the staff leaders in church to become a Christian. God the Holy Spirit saves and he knows our hearts. He is with the beggar on the street who calls out to him and the person at the altar. He is always holding out a free gift for all who would receive. Once you receive his gift, it is your responsibility to give it away. God commands every believer to be a witness.

There are many ways to share the plan of salvation, but the basic truths are the same. The Bible teaches that to receive salvation you must:

- Recognize your sin and confess that you are a sinner
- Be willing to turn from your sin
- Believe that God sent his only Son, Jesus, to live a perfect life on earth, and that he died on a cross for our sins and was raised three days later
- Receive Jesus to be your Lord and Savior

You must find a comfortable way to share the plan of salvation, and then pray and let the Holy Spirit take over.

He will guide your words, just as it says in 1 Corinthians 2:13: "This is what we speak, not in words taught by human wisdom but in words taught us by the Spirit, expressing spiritual truths in spiritual words."

ONE Focus Living Plan of Salvation

Over the years, I have been trained in many ways to share the plan of salvation: Christian Witness Training, marked New Testament, the Roman Road, FAITH, and others. I have personally trained over five hundred people to share the plan of salvation. My point is that there are countless ways to share the Gospel; you are the only one who can decide what is comfortable and natural for you.

The following example is usually the way I share Christ with others. First, I take time to ask them about their interests, family, work, or hobbies. Then I ask a question such as, "What do you understand it takes to get to heaven?" Most people will answer, "To be good enough." At that point, I will ask their permission to share how the Bible answers that question.

- Heaven is a gift from God.
  - "For God so loved the world that he gave his one and only Son, that whoever believes in him shall not perish but have eternal life" (John 3:16).
- This gift is given in response to our greatest need.
  - ". . . for all have sinned and fall short of the glory of God" (Rom. 3:23).
- Although we have earned spiritual death (separation from God), God offers this gift through his Son, Jesus Christ.

- o "For the wages of sin is death, but the gift of God is eternal life" (Rom. 6:23).
- Heaven is a free gift from God—we could *never* earn it.
    - o "For it is by grace you have been saved, through faith—and this is not from yourselves, it is the gift of God—not by works, so that no one can boast" (Eph. 2:8–9).
- Jesus is the only way to heaven.
    - o "Jesus answered, 'I am the way and the truth and the life. No one comes to the Father except through me'" (John 14:6).
- This gift of heaven can be yours if you receive Jesus by faith, inviting him into your heart and asking his forgiveness of your sin.
    - o "If you confess with your mouth 'Jesus is Lord,' and believe in your heart God raised him from the dead, you will be saved. For it is with your heart that you believe and are justified, and it is with your mouth that you confess and are saved" (Rom. 10:9–10).

Let this day become the greatest day in your life by receiving God's gift of heaven!

The Plan of Salvation and Children
Cindy

I have shared with children and youth in many settings. Usually it is one-on-one, but I have also shared with large groups during events such as vacation Bible school. Children are so innocent and eager to please, and therefore it is important to ask the Holy Spirit to guide my words as they attempt to understand at their own stage of maturity. It is vital that boys and girls seek Jesus with their hearts, not based on peer pressure or Mom and Dad waiting outside the door. The most important decision of their lives—total transformation—is not to be taken lightly, but in the same way it is not to be complicated. Jesus said, "I tell you the truth, anyone who will not receive the kingdom of God like a little child will never enter it" (Mark 10:15).

An example of a Gospel presentation follows.

Begin with prayer and then say, "I am here to talk to you about some good news and some bad news."

The Good News: Heaven

It is a beautiful place, better than anything you can imagine! It's even better than Disneyworld, or the beach, or . . . (let them give some suggestions). Heaven is perfect, a place with no sadness, sickness, or death. There are no bad things in heaven—no sin. The best thing about heaven is that God is there.

Does anyone know who God is? He is the creator of the world, and he made you, and he loves you—every part of you. He loves you so much that he even knows every hair on your head! "And even the very hairs of your head are all numbered" (Matt. 10:30).

The Bad News: Sin

Remember, I told you there is no sin in heaven. Well, all of us sin. I sin, you sin . . . your parents, your teachers, and even your pastors sin. Sin is anything God wouldn't like. It is disobeying God. If there can be no sin in heaven and we all sin, then how can we get there?

God made a way through his Son, Jesus. He sent Jesus to earth to be born as a baby, to grow up just like you and I did. But the difference in his life is that he never sinned. He never did *anything* wrong. He loved, healed, and served others, but people did not understand. Even though he lived a perfect life, he was nailed to a cross.

The Good News: Jesus Is Alive!

Three days after he was put in a tomb, Jesus rose from the grave, and he is alive today, preparing a place for us in heaven. Jesus died for our sins and made a way for us to get to heaven! Have you thought about becoming a child of God?

Becoming a Christian is like learning your ABCs:

A: Admit you are a sinner

B: Believe that Jesus is God's Son and that he died for your sins

C: Call on Jesus to be your Lord (your boss)

> **The Good News:**
> **Jesus Is Alive!**

Remember the Good News and the Bad News

- **Good news:** Heaven is a wonderful place where we can be with God, and there can be no sin in heaven.
- **Bad news:** We cannot get to God because we are sinners.
- **Good news:** Jesus died for our sins so we could have a way to God and heaven!

- **Bad news:** Not everyone goes to heaven because not all people accept Jesus as their Savior.
- **Good news:** When I accept Jesus as my Savior, I can tell others about Jesus so they can go to heaven, too!

Have you ever had a time when you asked Jesus into your heart to be your best friend and to save you from your sins? The Bible does not say, "When you are ten years old or twenty years old, you are ready to become a Christian." You will know when you are ready. There is a feeling provided by God's Holy Spirit that tells you when the time is right. Do not make a decision because your friend wants you to, or because your parents say it is time, or because you want to be baptized. Becoming a Christian is the most important decision you will make in your entire life. Wait until you know it is right.

Becoming a Christian takes responsibility. You are making a commitment to grow, learn, and share Jesus with others. It is also the greatest joy you will ever have. Having Jesus in your heart gives you a peace and comfort that is unexplainable. Even in the midst of trouble or crisis, you know you are not alone. God has told us, "Never will I leave you; never will I forsake you" (Heb. 13:5).

Where Is the Sinner's Prayer?

If you are ready to ask Jesus to be your Savior, you can pray something like this. It is not a prayer written in the Bible, but it is based on Bible verses:

Dear God, ("Everyone who calls on the name of the Lord will be saved." —Romans 10:13)

I have disobeyed your rules. ("For all have sinned and fall short of the glory of God." —Romans 3:23)

I believe Jesus died for my sins on the cross . . . (". . . that Christ died for our sins according to the Scriptures, that he was buried, that he was raised on the third day according to the Scriptures . . ." —1 Corinthians 15:3–4)

. . . and I receive him as my Lord, my best friend. ("Yet to all who received him, to those who believed in his name, he gave the right to become children of God." —John 1:12)

Forgive all my sins and give me a new, clean life. ("Blessed is the man whose sin the Lord will never count against him." —Romans 4:8)

Thank you for the gift of eternal life. ("For God so loved the world that he gave his one and only Son, that whoever believes in him shall not perish but have eternal life." —John 3:16)

If you become a child of God, celebrate! This is your spiritual birthday. Write down the date and celebrate this day every year. Now it is your responsibility to grow spiritually and get to know Jesus more and more. God's Word will help you each day, so let it be your instruction guide for life.

Witnessing to Family and Friends

Many say it is hardest to talk to family and friends about Christ because they know the "real you." They have seen your life before Christ. The positive side is that now they will have the chance to see a change in your heart and life.

There is already a relational bridge with family and friends, and they can see the progress as you give over areas of your life to Christ's control. Changes will become noticeable, and when this happens, you may find others starting to ask about your faith in Christ.

Do you feel inadequate about answering questions? Do not feel like you must become a Bible scholar. The only responsibility you have is to share what God has done for you and what you are learning each day. Don't worry—God does not expect you to be perfect, but he does expect you to grow and share his love with others.

How Do You Know When Someone Is Ready to Accept Christ?
Cindy

> *Yet to all who received him, to those who believed in his name, he gave the right to become children of God.*
> —John 1:12

As a children's minister, I have often had parents depend on me to determine if their child was ready to accept Christ as their Savior. Even though I was "trained," I still had doubts and fears when my own children came to that time of decision in their lives. I think the only thing we can do as parents, leaders, and friends is to depend on the Holy Spirit to guide us. Sometimes I use the following story to help explain how to know God is real:

One day, a young boy was asked the question, "How do you know God is there; how do you know he can be a part of your life?" The boy answered, "It's a lot like fishing. You can't see or hear the fish; you just feel him tugging on your line. I felt God tugging on my heart, and I asked him to come in."

The Lord is tugging on hearts all the time. Will you help your ONE realize that he or she can become a child of God? ONE Focus is simply about you showing and sharing the love of Christ, then letting God do the rest!

> **ONE Focus is simply about you showing and sharing the love of Christ, then letting God do the rest!**

ONE Focus Living

Over the years, God has blessed me with opportunities to see hundreds of people come into a relationship with him. There is nothing more special than helping another person trust Jesus as Lord and Savior, but here is a close second: seeing other Christians lead ONE to Christ for the first time! It never gets old to hear about a worship leader in Shreveport, Louisiana; a grandmother in Montgomery, Alabama; a teenager in Longview, Texas; a single mom in Lake Charles, Louisiana; a fifth grader in Broken Arrow, Oklahoma; a CEO in Flower Mound, Texas; a pastor in Macon, Georgia; or a brother in West Monroe, Louisiana, who shared Christ and welcomed another person into eternal salvation.

Every encounter with a ONE is actually a potential opportunity to change the course of that person's life and possibly the world. So what about you? Your ONE is waiting.

ONE Focus Challenge

Explaining the plan of salvation can be intimidating, no matter how strong your desire might be to minister to someone. If the idea of sharing the plan of salvation causes you great anxiety, you can practice explaining it to someone you are comfortable with, just as you practiced your testimony. More importantly, pray for God to give you peace and to speak through you, and trust that when the time comes, he will give you the words. As we have seen, Scripture and experience show us that God specializes in using the most unlikely and ordinary of instruments to accomplish his design!

Reflection

1. Do you remember when someone shared the plan of salvation with you? What did you feel, and what did you most want to know?

   _____

   _____

   _____

2. How close do you think your ONE is to being ready to accept "the greatest gift"? What obstacles do you think may still remain?

   _____

   _____

   _____

CHAPTER ELEVEN

Something to Celebrate

A Celebration of Life

Jenny LoBello

In November 2009 I attended a "Celebration of Life" service for a friend of mine who had died unexpectedly at the age of twenty-seven. All of us were in shock, but her life was definitely worth celebrating. There are very few people that you have known your whole life. I love the idea of God placing these special people in our lives . . . and sometimes we don't know why until that person is gone.

My friend Lauren was such a lively, confident person. She was always the life of the party, a friend to all. When she sang, it was like the voice of an angel. Lauren had a special gift for ministering to others. Although she had walked through some tough circumstances, she was selfless in the way she gave to others—Lauren's actions touched so many lives. For her family and friends, the celebration of Lauren's life goes on as people continue to come forward and share special things she did to minister to them. What a legacy!

One young woman wrote a story about how Lauren's life changed her, telling of how Lauren's actions and ministry came at the perfect time—right when she was ready to end her life. In another instance, as the family visited Lauren's gravesite, they met a woman who told them Lauren was there for her after the death of her husband when the medical bills had left her with nothing. There are so many "Lauren stories," and we could all learn from her. Lauren chose life and she chose to be joyful in whatever the world brought her way. She chose to smile at those she met, take time for people around her, and pray for the needs of others.

Lauren had such a good sense of humor. She was always pulling pranks, and her laughter could be heard from a mile away. Sometimes Lauren would sneak her sweet husband's cell phone away from him and set alarm messages to go off in the future. Several months after Lauren's death, her husband received a message on his phone from Lauren: "I love you! —Lauren." I know that she lit up the heavens with her laugh that day.

What will you choose to do for others? What legacy will you leave? Will your life be a celebration?

During the ONE Focus journey, celebration can come in many stages. For some believers, a step forward may be their commitment to participate in the Initiative. The next point might be to identify their ONEs, invite them to church, or have a spiritual conversation with them. Of course, the ultimate celebration is when ONE is brought to the saving knowledge of Jesus Christ. Do not forget to celebrate the joys along the way; many people who are committing to ONE Focus are rededicating their own lives to Christ. Celebrate—and celebrate often.

Both of our children are married with children, but we still celebrate their spiritual birthdays. We try to take them out to eat, and it is a great witnessing tool. When someone asks, "Whose birthday is it?" we respond with, "Oh, it is our child's spiritual birthday!" Then we get to explain what a spiritual birthday is. If you are a believer, remembering your commitment to God in this way accomplishes a couple of things. One is to celebrate—you were lost and now you will have eternal life. Another is to look back over the year and see if you have grown spiritually; where is the fruit of your witness and the stewardship of what God has given you?

> Celebrate—and
> celebrate often.

Personal success stories are very powerful and encourage others. If you have a story of celebration or an idea for serving your ONE, pass it on! The ONE Focus website is a great way to share prayer requests and stories. Visit us at www.onefocus.com.

Lost and Found

In Luke 15, Jesus tells three parables:

- "The Lost Sheep" (Luke 15:4–7):
  Suppose one of you has a hundred sheep and loses one of them. Does he not leave the ninety-nine in the

open country and go after the lost sheep until he finds it? And when he finds it, he joyfully puts it on his shoulders and goes home. Then he calls his friends and neighbors together and says, "Rejoice with me; I have found my lost sheep." I tell you that in the same way there will be more rejoicing in heaven over one sinner who repents than over ninety-nine righteous persons who do not need to repent.

- **"The Lost Coin" (Luke 15: 8–10):**
  Or suppose a woman has ten silver coins and loses one. Does she not light a lamp, sweep the house and search carefully until she finds it? And when she finds it, she calls her friends and neighbors together and says, "Rejoice with me; I have found my lost coin." In the same way, I tell you, there is rejoicing in the presence of the angels of God over one sinner who repents.

- **"The Prodigal Son" (Luke 15:11–32):**
  There was a man who had two sons. The younger one said to his father, "Father, give me my share of the estate." So he divided his property between them. Not long after that, the younger son got together all he had, set off for a distant country and there squandered all his wealth in wild living . . . (11–13)
  But while he was a long way off, his father saw him and was filled with compassion for him; he ran to his son, threw his arms around him and kissed him. The son said to him, "Father, I have

sinned against heaven and against you. I am not worthy to be called your son." But the father said to his servants, "Quick! Bring the best robe and put it on him. Put a ring on his finger and sandals on his feet. Bring the fattened calf and kill it. Let's have a feast and celebrate. For this son of mine was dead and is alive again; he was lost and is found." So they began to celebrate. (20–24)

Each parable ended with a verse containing a similar theme:

"I tell you that in the same way there will be more rejoicing in heaven over one sinner who repents than over ninety-nine righteous persons who do not need to repent" (Luke 15:7).

"In the same way, I tell you, there is rejoicing in the presence of the angels of God over one sinner who repents" (Luke 15:10).

"'For this son of mine was dead and is alive again; he was lost and now is found.' So they began to celebrate" (Luke 15:24).

In each parable, the "lost" (sheep, item, person) represents a sinner who needs to repent. The "found" (sheep, item, person) is the sinner who has repented. When the sinner repents, a glorious celebration takes place—the kind of party to which the angels are invited! That is a celebration I want to be a part of; how about you?

Angels rejoice when a sinner repents. There is an ongoing celebration for every person who was lost and is rescued.

> Jesus' plan is a ONE-by-ONE, person-by-person, individual initiative.

Jesus' plan is a ONE-by-ONE, person-by-person, individual initiative. ONE Focus fits right into that plan.

The Theme: Celebration When the Lost Come to Christ

Be imitators of God, therefore, as dearly loved children, and live a life of love, just as Christ loved us and gave himself up for us as a fragrant offering and sacrifice to God.
—Ephesians 5:1–2

It is important that we demonstrate the same attitude toward the lost as Jesus did. He welcomed them, sought them, and celebrated when they repented. When your ONE accepts Jesus as his or her personal Lord and Savior, it should be a memorable event. Here are some ideas for you and your ONE:

- Write down the date of their decision and celebrate it every year—this is your ONE's spiritual birthday! You might initiate the action with a birthday card and a cupcake celebration.
- Buy a new Bible, cross, or pendant to engrave with the date of decision and give it to your ONE.
- Encourage your ONE to write out how he or she came to know Christ and keep it in a Bible or journal.
- Invite your friends and family to attend your ONE's baptism. Suggest that your ONE invite these and others to attend.

- Take a picture of your ONE's baptism.
- Applaud the baptism. All too often we go crazy when our athletic team scores but sit silent when someone accepts Christ and follows through in the believer's baptism. Show your support!

Heaven Will Be a Celebration

In my Father's house are many rooms; if it were not so, I would have told you. I go to prepare a place for you. And if I go and prepare a place for you, I will come back and take you to be with me that you also may be where I am.
—John 14:2–3

What a great day it will be when Jesus welcomes us into heaven. We will enter a place with no more tears, pain, or suffering. It will be a place where the blind will see his face, the deaf will hear his voice, the lame will dance for joy, and the mute will sing praises to him (Isa. 35:5–6).

We don't know exactly what heaven will be like because the Bible doesn't tell us everything. We do get hints like, "No eye has seen, no ear has heard, no mind has conceived what God has prepared for those who love him" (1 Cor. 2:9). Sounds pretty good to me!

The details we do know about heaven are incredible. Christians have so much to look forward to. Share your excitement with others and give them the Good News— they can have eternal life, too!

What If Your ONE Does Not Respond?

Keep Giving Invitations—Patiently Endure

Dr. Michael Walker

Y ou have committed a full year to your ONE lost or unchurched friend. Be patient. Persevere. Persistence pays off. You do not have control over your ONE or the timing of your ONE's decision or lack thereof, but you do have control over your continuous endeavors to demonstrate Christ and his love.

The Bible overflows with verses on God's patient endurance:

James 1:12	God blesses those who patiently endure.
2 Peter 3:9	The Lord is not being slow about his promise, he is being patient for your sake. He does not want anyone to be destroyed.
Luke 8:15	Good soil patiently produces good harvest.
1 Peter 2:19	If you suffer for doing good and endure it patiently, God is pleased with you.
Ephesians 4:2	Be patient, bearing with one another in love.
Romans 8:2	We must wait patiently and confidently.
2 Timothy 2:24	Be patient with difficult people.

My favorite verses are the ones referring to his patient endurance over us. Jeremiah 33:11 reads, "His love endures forever," and Hebrews 12:2 reads, "Let us fix our eyes on Jesus, the author and perfecter of our faith, who for the joy set before him endured the cross, scorning its shame." Think of all the hostility he endured from sinful people, and then you won't become weary and give up.

He is still enduring today, patiently waiting on the many ONEs of the world to accept his love and forgiveness. I have a ONE who I have been inviting to a Bible study group since before ONE Focus existed. After weeks, months, and even years of patiently and weekly inviting him to attend, he asked, "When are you going to give up and quit asking me to come to your Bible group?"

My reply was, "When Jesus returns or whenever I die— whichever comes first."

Do not quit short of entrance to his Kingdom for your ONEs. They may never say yes, but you must never stop asking.

ONE Focus Challenge

Commit to celebrate every positive step along the journey of ONE Focus. Whether your ONE is just now opening up to share about life or is already on the road to developing a relationship with Jesus, trust that God has everything under control in his timing!

Share your celebrations with other believers. Your success will encourage them in their efforts. Be bold in your celebrating. After all, an approaching salvation and a new eternal life is worthy of excitement. Remember what your ONE is being saved to as well as saved from.

Reflection

1. What can you celebrate right now about your journey with your ONE and what God is doing in your ONE's life?

    _____

    _____

    _____

2. What can you celebrate that God is doing in your own life?

    _____

    _____

    _____

CHAPTER TWELVE

Leaving a Legacy

The Plan God Intended

It is always good to come back home to see family and friends. Recently, Cindy and I made a trip back to Louisiana for our granddaughter Jessa-Claire's one-year birthday party. While we were there, God used several situations to encourage me in our journey through ONE Focus.

On Saturday, I dropped Cindy off at a store to pick up a few last minute items for the party, and as I was going to park, I saw a gentleman who looked familiar. Stanley is a six-foot-five African-American man who stands out in any crowd, so I rolled down my window and shouted his name. Stanley turned, gave me that incredible smile of his, and came over to talk.

Stanley and I had attended the same school, and he briefly worked at First West on our building service team. I had not seen him for years, so he told me about his family and that he now had his own plumbing service. At the end of our conversation, I asked him how he was doing spiritually and he said, "I am good—you helped me with that a few years ago!" You see, Stanley was one of my ONEs. He told me he was a changed man and was involved in church.

On Sunday, I attended the worship service at First West, and it was a great experience. Dr. John Avant, the senior pastor, was concluding a new sermon series called "Meet My Friend." He was very gracious to recognize me in the service and acknowledge that their new initiative was building off the ONE Focus Initiative that began at First West a few years before. Dr. Avant is one of my favorite preachers and one of my biggest supporters and encouragers.

After the service, a lady I recognized stopped me and said she had led her ONE to the Lord two months ago. As I was leaving the building and walking across the parking lot, a van pulled up to me and another nice lady called my name. I went to the window, not knowing what to expect, and she said, "You may not know me, but my family and I were someone's ONEs." She pointed to the backseat of her van, introduced me to her daughters, and said one of them had accepted Christ.

I thank God every day for allowing me to be a small part of how God changes lives. ONE Focus is an initiative that keeps working because it is the plan God intended—ONE reaching ONE reaching ONE reaching ONE . . .

*All over the world this gospel is bearing fruit and growing,
just as it has been doing among you since the day you heard
it and understood God's grace in all its truth.*
—Colossians 1:6

What kind of legacy are you leaving behind in the places you worship, work, shop, take classes, play, or visit? What impact are you having on the lives of the people you meet?

> **What impact are you having on the lives of the people you meet?**

On and On

When you finish this book, ONE Focus does not stop. Once you have shared the love of Christ with others and see how it changes everything, you will never want to go back to life as usual! Finding another ONE will be a natural response. In fact, you may choose two, three, or more new ONEs. If your ONE has not accepted Christ, you can (and should) choose to continue showing God's love to that person, trust in God's timing, and hope that the seeds you are planting will one day bloom and grow.

When people commit to ONE Focus, their radar should always be looking for new ONEs. As one example, when Cindy and I first moved to the Dallas/Fort Worth area, everyone was a new face. A young man named Brian built our home, and he was a nice guy and was very helpful as we moved into the neighborhood. I began wondering about his spiritual condition, and over a few months I prayed for, encouraged, and showed appreciation to Brian for making the move into our home a good experience. He had other homes he was building, so he often stopped by or I would see him in the neighborhood.

After a while, I asked Brian about his spiritual condition, and his answer caught me off guard. He said, "I am a spiritual mutt." His mom was Jewish and his dad was Methodist. He mentioned that he had attended church a few times with his dad, but it was obvious he did not have a personal relationship with Jesus. I invited him to lunch so we could talk more and he agreed.

A few weeks later, I shared my story with Brian. I helped him understand the difference between religion and relationship. He was so open and humble when I asked him if he would like to put his faith and trust in Jesus. He did not hesitate and Brian became my brother in Christ. Within a few weeks, Brian took a new job in San Antonio and we lost touch. I thank God for that opportunity to share with him before he left!

I continue to receive ONE Focus testimonies. A pastor recently wrote to let me know that his thirteen-year-old daughter's ONE just gave her heart to Jesus. In another church, a son chose his mother and father as his ONEs, and now the whole family is attending church together.

There are many more stories, but remember, this is not the end; it is only the beginning.

The Next Step: Discipleship

The Bible teaches us that there is more to leaving a legacy than leading others to Christ. The early church was deeply involved with discipleship—developing strong Christians who would continue to grow in their faith and faith-driven actions.

There are two major parts to discipleship and both are critical. The first involves your personal development as a disciple of Jesus Christ. The second involves mentoring—or discipling—your ONE when your ONE comes to know Jesus.

> Discipleship—developing strong Christians who would continue to grow in their faith and faith-driven actions.

What Is a Disciple?

The word used for "disciple" in the Greek—*mathetes*—refers generally to a student, pupil, or apprentice. Other definitions for disciple are:

- One who is a follower of a master or spiritual teacher
- One who lives by the teachings and lifestyle of his or her master
- One who wants to emulate his or her master

A Christian disciple is one who accepts Jesus Christ as their personal Lord and Savior and assists in spreading the Good News of his salvation. Christian discipleship is the process by which disciples grow to be more like Christ in their everyday walk. Jesus himself defined his disciples as ones who knew the Word and were doers of the Word.

Discipleship Has a Cost

- Are you denying yourself?

*If anyone would come after me, he must deny
himself and take up his cross and follow me.*
—Matthew 16:24

We cannot put Jesus on a shelf and bring him out on Sunday or for Easter and Christmas. He must be the center of our lives at all times. If we truly commit ourselves to him, he must be our priority. It is not always easy, but it is always right. Once you begin changing your life to put Jesus first, it comes naturally. You will feel such a release from the burdens that were weighing you down. Try it; you will feel a new freedom!

- Are you abiding in him?

If you hold to my teaching, you are really my disciples.
—John 8:31

*If you remain in me and my words remain in you, ask
whatever you wish and it will be given to you.*
—John 15:7

God gave us a book that is "living and active" (Heb. 4:12). God's Word is alive and it gives energy; we all need his Word in our lives. In order to obey his commands, we must study the Bible to help us understand and grow. Just as a baby begins drinking milk before eating solid food, we progress from the basics to spiritual maturity.

Spending time alone with God is necessary to abide in him. If you have not established a daily quiet time, begin *now*. I know everyone is busy, so do not make excuses. If you are waiting until you "have it all together," that time will never come. God takes you as you are and gives you all you need. Hebrews 4:16 says we should come into his presence with confidence. He will welcome you!

Also be aware that isolation is not Christ's plan. Are you a part of a small group Bible study? Just remember that it is very important to fellowship with a body of believers and study God's Word together. I was in a men's group for over twenty-five years; now, the men may have changed over the years, but the group's purpose did not. We engaged each other in prayer, Bible study, encouragement, and accountability—all so we would be better disciples of Jesus.

- Are you willing to give up everything?

In the same way, any of you who does not
give up everything he has cannot be my disciple.
—Luke 14:33

I remember when God called us into the ministry. We put our house up for sale and prepared to move anywhere God called. Our children still talk about how they grew up wondering when we would come home and say, "God is leading us to minister at another church." It was not until our children were grown that God said, "It's time." Moving from West Monroe meant leaving our family, including a young granddaughter. It was one of the hardest things we have ever had to do, but we knew God had a plan. He blessed our small sacrifice—what he is looking for is a willing heart.

- Do you love others?

A new command I give you: Love one another. As I have
loved you, so you must love one another. By this will all men
know that you are my disciples, if you love one another.
—John 13:34–35

Paul referred to this as Christ's law. You must love others
and show it! Have we talked about that enough?

- Do you live by the Spirit?

But the fruit of the Spirit is love, joy, peace, patience,
kindness, goodness, faithfulness, gentleness, and self-control.
—Galatians 5:22

Before Jesus ascended into heaven, he promised the
disciples they would not be alone. "But the Counselor, the
Holy Spirit, whom the Father will send in my name, will
teach you all things and will remind you of everything I
have said to you" (John 14:26).

The Holy Spirit lives in each believer and wants to
produce spiritual fruit. As the believer becomes a disciple
and grows in Christ, the fruit develops. How do you produce
more fruit? Spend more time with the Gardener.

- Are you armed for battle?

Put on the full armor of God, so that when the day of evil
comes, you may be able to stand your ground.
—Ephesians 6:13

Stand firm then, with the belt of truth buckled
around your waist, with the breastplate of righteousness in
place, and with your feet fitted with the readiness that comes
from the gospel of peace. In addition to all this, take up the
shield of faith, with which you can extinguish all the flaming
arrows of the evil one. Take the helmet of salvation and
the sword of the Spirit, which is the word of God. And pray
in the Spirit on all occasions with all kinds of prayers and
requests. With this in mind, be alert and always
keep praying for all the saints.
—Ephesians 6:14–18

We are fighting an enemy and we must be prepared. God has provided a "suit of armor" to defend us against Satan and his attack. The catch is that we must use the armor correctly.

Putting on the armor can be done in your quiet time with the Lord. This special protection can prevent us from falling into temptation and giving in to the sin that pulls at us each day. Of course the armor cannot be seen, but it does help to visualize each piece as you "put it on."

> You are not called to be a reservist in God's army but an active warrior for Christ.

You are not called to be a reservist in God's army but an active warrior for Christ. Are you in the battle or are you a spectator? The lost are dying around you every second. Just remember: we are here to depopulate hell and populate heaven!

Lesson on Discipleship

Continue in what you have learned and
have become convinced of, because you know
those from whom you learned it, and how from infancy
you have known the holy Scriptures, which are able
to make you wise for salvation through faith in Christ
Jesus. All Scripture is God-breathed and is useful for teaching,
rebuking, correcting and training in
righteousness, so that the man of God may be
thoroughly equipped for every good work.
—2 Timothy 3:14–17

Discipleship also means that you are responsible for setting an example to other Christians, supporting each other through Christian love, fellowship, and correction. If your ONE comes to know Christ, you can disciple him or her by helping your ONE get started on a personal walk with Christ.

A great example of discipleship is the apostle Paul. He led a disciplined life and taught those lessons to others. In Paul's first letter to Timothy, he addresses the young pastor's responsibility to his church at Ephesus. Paul treats him like a son and gives him words of encouragement, wisdom, and warnings when needed. Here are a few of the instructions from Paul:

- Do not listen to gossip. (1 Tim. 4:7)
- Train yourself to be godly. (1 Tim. 4:7)
- Do not let anyone look down on you because you are young. (1 Tim. 4:12)

- Be an example in speech, in love, in faith, and in purity. (1 Tim. 4:12)
- Do not neglect your spiritual gifts. (1 Tim. 4:14)
- Be diligent in all matters. (1 Tim. 4:15)
- Watch your doctrine and your life closely. (1 Tim. 4:16)
- Treat others with respect: older men as your father, older women as your mother, younger men as your brothers, and younger women as your sisters. (1 Tim. 5:1–3)
- The love of money is the root of all kinds of evil. (1 Tim. 5:10)
- Pursue righteousness, godliness, faith, love, endurance, and gentleness. (1 Tim. 5:11)
- Fight the good fight of the faith. (1 Tim. 5:12)
- Take hold of the eternal life to which you were called. (1 Tim. 5:12)

Discipleship and Your ONE

After your ONE accepts Christ, he or she will need to begin the discipleship process. Remember, Christ's command is to go and make disciples, not just believers. Becoming a believer is the first step to discipleship, not the last. It is the beginning of a lifetime process, not the end. You do not have to be totally responsible, but because you have a relationship, you need to help your ONE get started in the right direction for baptism, small group participation, worship, and service. Check with your church staff to see if there are classes for new believers. Be careful not to intimidate your ONE, but demonstrate the importance of learning the basics.

A simple plan for new Christians is to tell them to take the word "PRAY" and use it as a reminder for directing spiritual growth.

P: Pray

R: Read your Bible

A: Attend church

Y: Yield to Christ each day

Continue in Faith

The book of Colossians is written by Paul to the faithful brethren in Christ who were in Colosse. His purpose is to show that Christ is to be first and foremost in everything and that the Christian's life should reflect that priority. Because believers are rooted in him, alive in him, and complete in him, it is inconsistent for them to live life without him. This lifestyle needs to *continue* in you, long after your first year of ONE Focus has gone by.

"Once you were alienated from God and were enemies in your minds because of your evil behavior. But now he has reconciled you by Christ's physical body through death to present you holy in his sight, without blemish and free from accusation—if you *continue* in your faith, established and firm, not moved from the hope held out in the gospel" (Col. 1:21–23, emphasis added).

The thirteenth chapter of Acts records this story of what happened when Paul and Barnabas were preaching in Antioch:

> "When the congregation was dismissed, many of the
> Jews and devout converts to Judaism followed Paul
> and Barnabas, who talked with them and urged

them to continue in the grace of God. On the next Sabbath, almost the whole city gathered to hear the word of the Lord" (Acts 13:43–44, emphasis added).

The next part of the story is not so great—the Jewish leaders got jealous because the whole town came to hear Paul, so they "talked abusively" about what Paul was saying. But did that stop the spreading of the Gospel? Acts 13:49 tells us, "The word of the Lord spread through the whole region."

What does this say to us? Continue in the grace of God and the Word of the Lord will spread through the whole region. We have a job to do! You and I have been reconciled to God through Jesus Christ, and now we must continue in our faith and share the hope of the Gospel.

May the God who gives endurance and encouragement give you a spirit of unity among yourselves as you follow Christ Jesus, so that with ONE heart and mouth you may glorify the God and Father of our Lord Jesus Christ.
—Romans 15:5–6

ONE Focus Challenge

If your ONE has accepted Christ, celebrate, and know that heaven is ringing with the applause of others celebrating with you. If your ONE has not yet reached that point, please consider continuing to love, pray for, and share with this person. God's timetable is not always ours—if God has placed this person on your heart, will you continue faithfully and trust in the Lord's timing?

You should also take time to celebrate the work that the Lord has done in you during this time, and to think about what God has revealed to you about his heart.

It is my prayer that you will continue to look for ONEs to reach around you, that you will view your life as an expression of Christ's love, and that as you do, you will experience even greater peace and joy as you come closer to the heart of the Father toward all of us. May your legacy be one of faith, hope, and love. God bless you as you reach the world by reaching ONE.

Reflection

1. If your ONE has not yet accepted God's plan for salvation, will you continue to minister to him or her?

   _____

   _____

   _____

2. What has God taught you through this book? Do you feel more equipped to share the Gospel with others?

   _____

   _____

   _____

3. What kind of legacy do you want to leave behind, and how can you make this a reality?

   _____

   _____

   _____

CHAPTER THIRTEEN

The Next Chapter

The story doesn't end here. The rest of the book is yours to write—the pages are blank, and it's up to you to fill them. Will you continue seeking to share God's love with the people around you every day? Will you keep pursuing your ONE, or if your ONE has accepted Christ, find a new ONE to serve? Will you follow through on what you have learned from this book and, more importantly, from the Book—God's Word?

There is another book as well, a book that is waiting for names to be entered into it of all the ones who hear and believe.

He who overcomes will, like them, be dressed in white.
I will never blot out his name from the book of life, but will
acknowledge that name before my Father and his angels.
—Revelation 3:5

The pages are yours to fill. The question is this: will you make a difference? Will *you* be different? What will the pages of your chapter—or the story of your life—have to say?

_____

_____

_____

_____

_____

_____

_____

_____

_____

_____

_____

_____

_____

_____

_____

_____